TALES OF MEXICAN CALIF

COSAS DE CALIFORNIA

by *Señor* Don Antonio Franco Cor
ancient resident of the City of Los Angeles

A work in which the author relates the particulars of what occurred in the southern parts during the years of 1846-1847, giving also some idea of manners and customs.

Dictated to Mr. Thomas Savage for H. H. Bancroft, 1877
and now in the Bancroft Library, University of California, Berkeley

Translated by Diane de Avalle-Arce

Edited by Doyce B. Nunis, Jr., Professor Emeritus of History
University of Southern California

Illustrations by
Alan Archambault

Old Glory captured, see page 41.
Covers: the author by Alexander
Harmer, c. 1880, and back, the
author's house; Los Angeles Co.
Museum of Natural History.

INTRODUCTION

Hubert Howe Bancroft (1832-1918), a native of Ohio, came to California from New York State in 1852. After trying his hand at mining, he began to sell books, a trade he had first entered in Buffalo. He journeyed east in 1855 to purchase additional stock and materials for a new business. Returning to San Francisco in 1856, he opened a combination book shop and stationery store. Two years later he expanded into printing and publishing, ranging across the entire spectrum of that field of activity. He prospered.

In 1859, fascinated by the history of the Pacific Coast, Mexico, and Central America, he began to collect materials as a basis for writing a massive history of the regions mentioned. He acquired books, pamphlets, manuscripts, maps, newspapers, periodicals, everything he could lay his hands on pertaining to his planned historical work. The end product totaled thirty-nine huge volumes. Contained within that massive accomplishment, usually referred to as *Bancroft's Works*, was his seven-volume *History of California*, along with two companion volumes, *California Pastoral* and *California Inter Pocula*.

To augment the historical resources he had gathered to prepare these volumes, Bancroft introduced a novel idea. He hired a number of assistants as researchers, writers, and editors. In addition, he hired a small group of men to visit early California pioneers still living in the last half of the nineteenth century. These field assistants undertook to interview important old timers and take down their recollections. These collected interviews were called dictations by Bancroft.[1]

They were the forerunner of the contemporary practice of oral history where individuals are interviewed and recorded by tape and/or video recorders. Such memoirs or recollections are a vital source of firsthand historical knowledge and are an invaluable source of information to be found nowhere else but in people's memories.[2]

Among the many dictations Bancroft's assistants collected was *Cosas de California* (Tales of California), by Antonio Franco Coronel. When his dictation was completed on November 16, 1877, Coronel penned the following letter to "Señor Don H. H. Bancroft, San Francisco":

"My very dear Sir. The arduous and gigantic enterprise you have in your hands I hardly imagine will profit you materially. But I am sure your name will go down to posterity as a genius among historians.

"This little memoir and product of a feeble recollection I hope will be useful to you in some fashion. If such be the case I am entirely satisfied and recompensed.

"Your servant, respectfully,

A.F. Coronel"

Bancroft was wise in asking Coronel for his recollections, for he had played an integral part in California's history from his arrival in the Mexican territory as a sixteen-year-old youth in 1834. Born in Mexcio City, October 21, 1817, Coronel was the first son of Ignacio Coronel and Francisca Romero. He was the couple's second-born child, the elder being a sister, Jesefa, two years Coronel's senior. Later the family would grow to include two more daughters and another son, Manuel.

On August 1, 1834, the Coronel family, including the five children, sailed for California on the *Morelos* as members of the second contingent of the Padrés-Híjar party. They had been recruited as members of the Cosmopolitan Company, a colonizing venture supported by the Mexican government to augment the population of California as an added precaution against possible Russian advance southward from Unalaska and adventurers from the United States. In the bargain, the Russians had illegally occupied a tract of land north of San Francisco above Bodega Bay on the Pacific Ocean, where they had established an agricultural colony and built Fort Ross. Russian encroachment on California territory was a worrisome prospect to the Mexican government. The Padrés-Híjar party was mounted as a deterrent to that challenge. In addition, the party included a number of educated and talented individuals who would enhance life in California.[3]

In his dictation, Coronel tells us much about his life from his family's joining the Padrés-Híjar party down through the gold rush, spanning the years 1834-1850. He also relates some of the early history of Los Angeles, especially criminal and vigilante activities in that raw frontier town of the 1850s. Lastly, he contributes an invaluable recounting of the California missions in his time, as well as the customs indigenous to Californios, a term meaning native-born, Spanish-speaking Californians. Let his "Tales of California" describe those aspects of his life and times.

Coronel adjusted well to California life after statehood. He did have one major setback, however. His Rancho Cañada atras de los Verdugos, sometimes called the Sierra de los Verdugos in Los Angeles County, situated back of the present-day towns of La Cañada and La Crescenta, granted in 1846, was declared invalid by the U.S. Land Commission. That was a blow, financially. His father's land titles also suffered. Ignacio Coronel had received four land grants from the Mexican government: Rancho Cañada, 1843, in the vicinity of his son's rejected claim, which was lost and patented to another in 1866; Rancho Corralitos, Santa Cruz County at Corralitos, which he occupied in 1836, but which was granted to José Amesti in 1844; Rancho Sierra de Cucamonga, San Bernardino County near Alta Loma, which was never patented; and the Rancho Cajón de los Negros, also in San Bernadino County at Cajón, granted in 1846, but subsequently claimed by an American settler. Thus at his death in 1862, Ignacio Coronel had no land to pass on to his eldest son and heir.[4]

But this does not mean Coronel was not well off. Indeed, he was a very prosperous citizen. From his mining days he amassed enough capital to purchase 670 acres (53 acres were in the then city limits) on Alameda Street in Los Angeles and laid out a splendid orchard and vineyard. He gained an enviable reputation as an orchardist and vineyardist and was an active member of the State Horticultural Society, serving on its board from 1884-1885. He was among the first to have an orange grove, some 1,000 trees, a harbinger of the southern California citrus industry.[5]

After California statehood, Coronel renewed his interest in politics, joining the Democratic party. As a result, he held several appointive and elected offices. From 1850-1853 he was county assessor. In 1853 he was elected mayor of Los Angeles, a one-year term, followed by service on the City Council, 1854-1867 (with a two-year hiatus), a ten-year period of public service, including the presidency of the Council, 1857-1858. He was appointed to the first Los Angeles Board of Health, January 1, 1862, and served again, 1879-1882. He capped his political career by election as State Treasurer, serving a single four-year term, 1867-1871.

It was not until December 18, 1873, that Coronel married. His bride was thirty-seven-year-old Mariana Williamson of Los Angeles, a lady who had been educated by the Sisters of Charity. The groom was fifty-six. Mrs. Coronel's father was from Maine; his wife was a native of Mexico. Coming from that bilingual background, Mrs. Coronel was fluent both in English and Spanish. Although they had no children, theirs was a happy marriage from all accounts.[6] One source noted, "The union has been a singularly happy one. All those who have known them with any degree of intimacy have been struck with the perfect sympathy which seems to exist between them."[7]

Their home became a center of maintaining the traditions and culture of old California, in particular music and dance. A telling description was recorded by Helen Hunt Jackson. She wrote:

"Occasionally at the last moment Don Antonio would take up his guitar, and, in a voice still sympathetic and full of melody, sing an old Spanish love song, brought to his mind by thus living over the events of his youth. Never, however, in his most ardent youth could his eyes have gazed on his fairest sweetheart's face with greater devotion than that which now rest on the noble, expressive countenance of his wife, as he sings the ancient, tender strains."[8]

The couple took up residence in "one of the old pueblo adobes... and there they were visited by Helen Hunt Jackson when she came here [to Los Angeles] in the early eighties." The Coronels moved again in 1886 opposite the home "that Coronel built on the southwest corner of Seventh Street and Central Avenue." A contemporary wrote that "Mrs. Coronel was a recognized leader in local society, proving very serviceable in the preparation of *Ramona* and receiving, in return, due acknowledgement from the distinguished authoress [Helen Hunt Jackson] who presented her with the first copy of the book published [in 1884]."[9]

"The Coronel's contribution to that famous novel set in southern California is best described by a contemporary who knew the facts firsthand. This early historian of Los Angeles recorded that Mrs. Jackson, not long after her arrival in Los Angeles to spend the winter of 1881-1882, "met Antonio F. and Doña Mariana Coronel; and finding the latter a highly intelligent and affable lady, she passed some hours each day at the hospitable Coronel mansion, driving out from her hotel and reclining under the broad palms."

At first, Mrs. Coronel was suspicious of the eastern visitor's motives, but that initial "distrust was dispelled by the warmth of the author's personality." With rapport established,

"... Doña Mariana, opening both her house and heart, contributed inestimably to the success of the now famous *Ramona*, most of the rough notes for which were written at a little table on the Coronel veranda. On Doña Mariana's advice, Mrs. Jackson selected the Del Valle ranch house at the Camulos (near present-day Newhall) as the best-preserved and most typical place for a background; although, disappointed in not finding the Del Valles at home, and consequently seeing the imagined headquarters of Ramona for but an hour or two, she was compelled to rely upon her Los Angeles hostess for many of the interesting and singularly accurate details."[10]

When Mrs. Jackson returned to the East, she wrote "a charming description of life at the old Coronel adobe." She provides this graphic description of the Coronel home:

"In the western suburbs of Los Angeles is a low adobe house, built after the ancient style, on three sides of a square, surrounded by orchards, vineyards, and orange groves, and looking out on an old-fashioned garden, in which the southernwood, rue, lavender, mint, marigolds, and gillyflowers hold their own bravely, growing in straight and angular beds among the newer splendors of verbenas, roses, carnations, and geraniums. On two sides of the house runs a broad porch, where stands rows of geraniums and chrysanthemums growing in odd-shaped earthen pots."

Much taken with the beauty of the setting of the Coronel's home, Mrs. Jackson observed, "whoever has the fortune to pass as a friend across the threshold of this house finds himself transported, as by a miracle into the life of a half-century ago." She noted, "the rooms are ornamented with fans, shells, feather and wax flowers, pictures, saints' images, old laces, and stuffs, in the quaint gay Mexican fashion." On her first visit, she was also struck by the fact that each room was "brilliant with bloom. In every one of the deep window-seats stood a cone of bright flowers, its base made by large white datura blossoms, their creamy whorls all turned outward, making a superb decoration." Although she went on a brief courtesy call for just a few minutes, she "stayed three hours, and left carrying...bewildering treasures of pictures of the olden [Californio] times."[11]

She described Mrs. Coronel as "a beautiful young Mexican woman," with "clear olive skin, soft brown eyes, delicate sensitive nostrils, and broad smiling mouth, all... of the Spanish madonna type..." Sometimes, "when her low brow is bound, as is often her wont, by turban folds of soft brown or green gauze, her face becomes a picture indeed."

As for Don Antonio, Mrs. Jackson waxed eloquent about this "gray-headed Mexican señor":

"Don Antonio speaks little English; but the señora knows just enough of the language to make her use of it delicious, as she translates for her husband. It is an entrancing sight to watch her dark weather-beaten face, full of lightning changes as he pours out torrents of his nervous, eloquent Spanish speech... He is sixty-five years of age, but he is young: the best waltzer in Los Angeles to-day; his eye keen, his blood fiery quick; his memory like a burning-glass bringing into sharp light and focus a half-century as if it were yesterday..."

Mrs. Jackson also caught the fact that that Don Antonio, although he did not speak English, apparently understood it well for occasionally he would interrupt his wife's translation with "No, no; that is not it." She could not fathom, however, why he chose not to use English, but suspected it swas due to his looking "back to the lost empire of his race and people on the California shores with a sorrow far too proud for antagonisms or complaints." Although reconciled to the inexorableness of events and intellectually sympathetic to progress, reform, and the advancement of civilization, in "his heart...[he was] none the less saddened and lonely."[12]

One special thing which caught Mrs. Jackson's eye was a "little southeast room" in which Don Antonio kept "the relics of the time when he and his father were foremost representatives of ideas and progress in the City of the Angels, and taught the first school kept in the place." The room was full, maps and charts hanging on the wall; "old atlases, primers, catechisms, grammars, reading-books," as well as "elaborate instructions for teachers and schools" based on the old Lancaster system which was in vogue in the 1830s. In addition there were other Spanish-language books in the library, among them volumes on Spain's laws for military judges (1781): "a quaint old volume called 'Secrets of Agriculture, Fields and Pastures,'" written in 1617 and published in 1781, a "sure guide to success with crops," in addition to histories, almanacs, arithmetics, "dating back to 1750." Also on hand were multiplication tables, drawing books, and music, including "music of the first quadrilles ever danced in Mexico...a ragged pamphlet, which, no doubt, went gleeful rounds in the City of the Angels for many a year." In addition to the library and school materials, Coronel had "bundles of records of the branding of cattle at San Gabriel Mission" and a host of other historical and ethnological artifacts.[13]

With her visit concluded, Mrs. Jackson never left the premises without being showered with gifts. Upon her departure, she wrote, "The señora never allowed me to depart without bringing to me, in the carriage, farewell gifts of flowers and fruits; clusters of grapes, dried and fresh; great boughs full of oranges, more than I could lift. As I drove away thus, my lap filled with bloom and golden fruit, canopies of golden fruit over my head..."

Thus it was that Mrs. Jackson "spent many an afternoon" listening to Don Antonio's tales of life and adventure in California. As sunset approached the time arrived for her return to Los Angeles in her carriage. Mrs. Jackson's praise of Don Antonio reached a national audience in the readership of her writings.[14]

Not only a leading political figure in the community, Coronel was also prominent in the cultural life of Los Angeles. Along with other Californios he continued to maintain their past traditions. It had long been the custom to visit and entertain in one's home. As one observer noted when the *fandango* was much in vogue, Coronel "...and other native Californians were among its most noted exponents." This favorite form of entertainment, dancing, often led to the hiring of a hall for the gala occasion. The sponsors of the event:

"...did not hesitate to take the leading parts [in the dances], and turned the whole proceeds over to the church or charity. On such occasions not merely the plain people...were the *fandangeros*, but the flower of society turned out *en masse*, adding to the affair a high degree of *éclat*. There was no end, too, of good things to eat and drink...and the enjoyment was not lessened by the fact that every such dance hall was crowded to the walls, and the atmosphere, relieved by but a narrow door and window or two, was literally thick with dust and smoke."[15]

In addition to maintaining the cultural traditions of the Californios' way of life, Coronel was also active in promoting the welfare of his fellow citizens. He took a lively interest in education and was one of the group of citizens who founded the Los Angeles public school system in 1853 and later a public library. He also served as a school commissioner in 1855. In 1856 he was one of the committee and contributors responsible for bringing the Sisters of Charity to the city. The Sisters in turn established southern California's first orphanage, school for girls, and hospital. Coronel, in 1865, was a member of a three-man committee appointed by Bishop Thaddeus Amat to raise funds for the construction of a permanent facility for St. Vincent's College, the first institution of higher learning in Los Angeles. Established by the Jesuits in temporary headquarters in 1855, a decade later, larger space needs had to be met. The fund drive was successful, and a newly constructed two-story building on Sixth Street, between Broadway and Hope, was ready to house the institution in the spring of 1867. Lastly, Coronel was active in the Spanish American Benevolent Society, a charitable organization which assisted needy Spanish-speaking residents.[16]

Another activity which engaged Coronel's attention was the founding of the Historical Society of Southern California in November-December 1883. He was a charter member of that society, which still exists today. Known for his collection of historical materials and artifacts, on one occasion Coronel hosted a Society meeting at his home to display select items from the collection. One of the participants present at that meeting recalled:

"Three hundred guests assembled to enjoy the proverbial Spanish hospitality of this distinguished couple... Don Antonio possessed...valuable historical and ethnological collections; and some of his choice curios were that evening placed at the service of the guests. [The Society president]...presid[ed] at a table once used by the first Constitutional Governor, [José] Echeandía, and I still recall the manner in which Antonio chuckled when he told us how he had swapped 'four gentle cows' for the piece of furniture; while, instead of a gavel, Señora Coronel had provided a bell long used to summon the Indians to Mission service."[17]

Years later, what remained of Coronel's collection was given to the Los Angeles County Museum of Natural History.[18]

Coronel died near midnight on April 16-17, 1894. He and his wife had visited the 1893 Chicago World's Fair, but their trip was cut short by the illness which eventually claimed his life. One of his eulogists provided an intimate insight into Coronel's many contributions to his state, writing:

"Mr. Coronel, in his lifetime, made a most honorable record as a friend of the defenceless Mission Indians of Southern California. Of this fact Mrs. Helen Hunt Jackson has borne warm testimony in several national publications... He gave to Mrs. Jackson the materials of her story of *Ramona* published in 1884, and aided her in many ways in acquiring a knowledge of the customs and traditions of the people of the country, necessary to give characteristic coloring of the story [ably assisted by his wife]...He also gave her the data of the account of Friar Junípero Serra, the venerable founder and first president of the California Missions. Mr. Coronel also took an active part...in the restoration of San Carlos Mission [at Monterey], and in the solemnization of the centennial, in 1884, of the death of Junípero Serra."[19]

Coronel was buried in Calvary Cemetery on April 17 after a requiem mass in St. Vibiana's Cathedral offered by his longtime friend, Father Joachim Adam, vicar general of the Los Angeles Diocese and rector of the cathedral. [20]

Coronel, however, continues to live in his memoirs, *Tales of California*, dictated in Spanish to Thomas Savage in late 1877, now translated in full for the first time into English. [21] A contemporary historian who knew the pioneer Californio remarked: "In the many conversations [with him] ... concerning the past history of California, and especially of the part he took in it, I have been impressed with the vividness of his recollections; and I have felt that a record merely of those personal recollections would, to a certain extent, constitute a history of California."[22]

Bancroft has this to say of Coronel: "He is a man of acknowledged ability, as well as a useful citizen." Commenting on his dictation, the historian wrote:

"...From him I obtained several valuable papers regarding his father and himself, and in 1877 he dictated for me his *Cosas de California*. This is a folio volume of 265 pages, full of valuable material...The whole book is full of valuable matter related in a clear and pleasant style, free from exaggeration or bias."[23]

Generous praise, indeed, for Bancroft was noted for his frankness.

Sad to say, no one has yet written a detailed biography of Coronel. The first step along those lines was undertaken by Mercedes May Sparks in her study *Don Antonio Franco Coronel: His Relation to the Growth and Development of California*, completed in 1931.[24] The second such biographical effort was by Frederico A. Sanchez in his

Antonio F. Coronel, a Californio and a Ranchero: His Life and Times in Mexican Alta California, 1834-1850.[25] However, the latter study is based extensively on Coronel's dictation and ends, as indicated, with the year 1850, while the former is based mostly on secondary sources.

Although Coronel's memory on the whole is quite accurate, like all of us except the publisher herewith, he occasionally makes mistakes. Where he has a lapse of memory, corrections have been supplied in footnotes. Here and there his narrative has been annotated in order to assist the reader to a better understanding of what Coronel is referring to in his dictation. The text has been translated ably by Diane de Avalle-Arce who adhered closely to the original narrative in order to keep Coronel's language his own. Where additions to his textual narrative and/or translating comments are supplied, such intrusions are inserted in brackets.

Readers interested in identifying the numerous individuals Coronel mentions in his dictation will find most of those names in the "Pioneer Register" in Bancroft's *History of California,* at the end of Volume II-V, arranged in alphabetical order. This biographical dictionary has also been reprinted as a separate volume under the title, *Register of Pioneer Inhabitants of California, 1542-1848* (Los Angeles, 1964) and a like volume that same year was published in Baltimore, Maryland.

Now, turn to the first page and begin to relive the story of California from the days of Mexican rule to early American statehood. What follows is that fascinating history revealed by an individual who lived through those extraordinary decades that saw California move from a Mexican pastoral province to the thirty-first state in the Union, a saga vividly recalled for us by Antonio Franco Coronel.

Mimi and Sibyl Knill,
senior editors

John Knill,
publisher

The author   H. H. Bancroft
the Great   Prof. Nunis

NOTES TO THE INTRODUCTION

1 For his work and life, see John W. Caughey, *Hubert Howe Bancroft, Historian of the West* (Berkeley and Los Angeles, 1946).

2 Two useful books on this subject are: Willia K. Baum, *Transcribing and Editing Oral History* (Nashville, 1977) and Barbara Allen and Lynwood Montell, *From Memory to History: Using Oral History Sources in Local History Research* (Nashville 1981). Also useful is Brad Jolly, *Videotaping Local History* (Nashville, 1982).

3 For an excellent history, see G. Alan Hutchinson, *Frontier Settlement in Mexican California: The Padrés-Híjar Colony, and Its Origins, 1769-1835* (New Haven, 1969).

4 Robert G. Cowan, *Ranchos of California* (Fresno, 1956), Nos. 77, 124, 138, 271, 659.

5 [Thomas H.] Thompson and [Albert A.] West, *History of Los Angeles County, California* (Reprint of 1880 ed.; Berkeley, 1959), pp. 176, 187.

6 Biographical data drawn from H[enry] D. Barrows, "Antonio F. Coronel," *Annual Publication Historical Society of Southern California*, V, Pt. I (1900): 78-82; *The Antonio F. Coronel Collection* (Los Angeles, 1906), pp. 5-6; Marco R. Newmark, "Antonio Franco Coronel," *Quarterly Historical Society of Southern California*, XXXVI (1954): 161-162; J[ames] M. Gwinn, *Historical and Biographical Record of Los Angeles and Vicinity* (Chicago, 1901), pp. 531-532; Hubert H. Bancroft, *History of California* (7 vols., San Francisco, 1884-1890), II: 768, who mistakenly uses Francisco rather than Franco for Coronel's middle name.

7 *An Illustrated History of Los Angeles County* (Chicago, 1889), p. 428.

8 Helen Hunt Jackson, "Echoes in the City of the Angels," *Century Magazine*, XXVII (1883-84): 210.

9 Harris Newmark, *Sixty Years in Southern California, 1853-1913*, ed. by Maurice H. and Marco R. Newmark (4th ed., Los Angeles, 1970, 1970), pp. 444-445.

10 *Ibid.*, pp. 530-531.

11 *Ibid.*, p. 531. For a discussion of the role played by the Coronels in assisting Helen Hunt Jackson with background material for her famed novel, *Ramona*, see Ruth Odell, *Helen Hunt Jackson* (New York, 1937), pp. 174-177.

12 The article was entitled "Echoes in the City of the Angels" and appeared in the December 1884 issue of *Century Magazine*. It was subsequently reprinted in two of Mrs. Jackson's books, *Glimpses of Three Coasts* (Boston, 1886), pp. 103-141, and in *Glimpses of the California Missions* (Boston, 1902), pp. 161-209. I have relied on the last title for the references which follow. The quote cited in the text is from *ibid.*, pp. 192-193.

13 *Ibid.*, pp. 193-194.

14 *Ibid.*, pp. 194, 197-198, 206, 209.

15 Newmark, *Sixty Years*, p. 135.

16 *Ibid.*, pp. 105, 190, 660*n*; Thompson and West, *History of Los Angeles County*, p. 72; Newmark, "Antonio Franco Coronel," p. 162.

17 Newmark, *Sixty Years*, p. 604.

18 Helen Hunt Jackson describes some of this collection in *Glimpses of the California Missions*, pp. 197-199. A catalogue of the collection was prepared by the Los Angeles Chamber of Commerce when it was presented to that organization by Coronel's widow.

19 Barrows, "Antonio F. Coronel," p. 81.

20 Book of Deaths, I: No. 1019, April 17, 1894, St. Vibiana Cathedral Rectory, Los Angeles.

21 Nellie Van de Grift Sanchez translated a portion of Coronel's "Tales of California," that portion dealing with Californio customs, which was published under the title "Things Past" in *Touring Topics*, September 1931.

22 Barrows, "Antonio F. Coronel," p. 82.

23 Hubert H. Bancroft, *California Pastoral* (San Francisco, 1888), pp. 778-779.

24 Master's Thesis, University of Southern California, 1931.

25 Doctoral Dissertation, University of Southern California, 1982. 2 vols.

[f 1] [marginalia] Begin Nov. 2

[I]

Antonio Franco Coronel, resident of the property known as Coronel's Mansion, about a mile south of the city of Los Angeles, came to California with his parents Don Ignacio Coronel and Doña Francisca Romero de Coronel and several brothers and sisters.

We arrived as part of the Híjar and Padrés colony in 1834, on the warship *Morelos* commanded by Don Lucas Manso, landing in Monterey.[1] My worthy father held the position of head schoolmaster of the colony.

We stayed some time in Monterey during the dispute between General Figueroa and Don José María Híjar with regard to the civil command of the territory.

Señor Híjar was both civil leader and director of the colony, and Señor José María Padrés was both military commander and vice-director.[2]

Padrés was a native of Puebla and closely associated with my family since a child. I was an intimate friend of his sisters, [f 2] brothers and cousins. His parents, who were skilled workers, had died, and the family lived in great poverty. Padrés dedicated himself to his education, first primary school, then mathematics and other branches of military engineering. All this time my parents helped him along as much as they could, as a cadet and then as an ensign in the Corps of Engineers. When he had attained this rank — or possibly that of lieutenant — he first went to California with Lieutenant Colonel Echeandía, the governor.

He was with Echeandía for his term of office. Like his superior, he was a man of extreme republican and liberal ideas which he imparted to the young men of the principal families of the territory. This aroused the antagonism of the old Spanish friars, who were monarchists and absolutists of the old school.

During his stay in California Padrés devoted himself to the study of the geography [f 3] and topography of the country, and its resources. He was the first to publish in Mexico the facts about the mineral and agricultural wealth of California, and its climate. He predicted a brilliant future for the territory, as the most fertile, rich and healthful in the whole Republic.

The arrival of Don Manuel Victoria in 1831 to replace Echeandía changed the situation. As I said before, Padrés's progressive ideas and his influence on the younger generation were anathema to the friars; they promptly dominated Victoria's policies. In consequence, Padrés, who had been an assistant inspector of troops, was unable to remain in the country. Victoria shipped him back to Mexico.[3]

From that time on, he dedicated himself exclusively to organizing [f 4] a colony to emigrate to California, and warning the central government to take action before it lost "the most precious pearl in Mexico's crown," as he prophetically feared.

Even before the colony was organized, under the auspices of the Cosmopolitan Company, Padrés was incessantly recruiting families for California, my own among

13

them. He also tried to get the government to send political exiles on the theory that it would be good for the exiles and good for the country. In consequence, when the colonists arrived, there were several political exiles among them. These were decent people of good social position who for purely political reasons had run afoul of the government and were punished as severely as though they were criminals. There were also a few [f 5] opponents of the dictator Santa Anna, escaping political persecution. [4]

In 1832 or 1833, Don Juan Bandini went to Mexico as California's delegate to the National Congress. A progressive like Padrés, also determined to develop the territory, he was a powerful ally for the colonial dream.[5]

Together they achieved their goal. It was also helpful that the vice-president and acting executive, Gómez Farías, was a strong liberal and took a lively interest in the project.[6]

Approved by Congress, the Convent of San Camilo in Mexico City was appointed for the [f 6] colonists to gather. The interest and enthusiasm was so great that if the government had had the money, it could have sent to California more than a thousand families of moderate social status who understood the advantage of emigrating.

Common Mexicans in their ignorance believed California was impossibly remote, populated for the most part by barbarous Indians called *Mecos*; anyone fool enough to go there was sure to suffer great trials and fall victim to savages.

When the colonists were ready to set out in covered wagons and the coaches of well-off families, some of the mob tried to stop them from leaving; [f 7] but the wagons were escorted by armed and mounted colonists, and the government provided a squadron of cavalry.

We journeyed through the Republic without any more obstacle than lack of money, which delayed us in Guadalajara and Tepic. Señor Híjar had to mortgage his handsome estate near Guadalajara in order to cover the expenses of the expedition.[7] From Tepic we went to San Blas, where we found the corvette *Morelos*, also the bark *Natalia* which belonged to a company of the colonists; it was said that the *Natalia* was the self-same ship in which the Emperor Napoleon I escaped from Elba in 1815.[8]

Most of the single men and skilled workers boarded the *Natalia*. Also travelling on it were Híjar, Buenaventura Araujo, Horacio Serrano, Argüello, et. al.[9] The government employees [f 8] and their families embarked on the corvette, including Padrés, Don Luis del Castillo Negrete, a lawyer, Don Zenón Fernández and Don Ignacio Coronel and their families, the *licenciado* Romero, Mariano Bonilla and his two brothers, Agustín Olvera, José Abrego and others whose names I don't remember now.[10]

At sea we endured a terrible storm. The tiller was lashed, the sails taken in and furled, the fire doused; everyone was kept on rations of ship's biscuit and cheese for four days. We almost wrecked on Point Conception in the high winds, and were saved by a miracle. All the passengers were below decks except a boy named Vidal and myself; we happened to be in the bows looking at the storm, because we had already picked up a lot of seamanship. The second in command, Lieutenant Azcona, [f 9] was the watch officer. Captain Manso, who had never navigated this coast before, had been on deck a short while before and told Azcona to keep good watch, because we were very near land.

Soon after Manso went to his cabin, Vidal pointed out to me a rock just visible in the thick mists. I yelled "Land ho!" to Azcona, who might have seen the rock at the same moment I yelled. He immediately ordered a change of course and all hands on deck. The sailors turned out and almost all the passengers helped to work the ship, finally reaching safety after a near escape which frightened us all very much. Luckily, the ladies didn't realize the danger at the time, only believing we were getting to the end of the voyage.

But after the storm we were becalmed for four or five days, finally reaching the port of [f 10] Monterey the 24th of September, Feast of Our Lady of Mercy, if I'm not mistaken.

Monterey was too small to have lodging houses, but as soon as news of our arrival got around, the residents decided to parcel out among their houses the families in the corvette; they went right down to the beach to receive us and take us home with them. There were a few empty rooms in the Presidio where some families were billeted as well. We had a friendly and hospitable reception on all sides.

The first news we had was that General Santa Anna had sent a special messenger overland with new orders for General Figueroa not to transfer military or civil powers. This gave rise to a dispute between Figueroa and Padrés on the one hand, and with Híjar on the other.

[f 11] The upshot of it was that Híjar and Padrés were stripped of office, except as directors of the colony under the command of General Figueroa.[11] They were assigned Sonoma as the place to settle, and Figueroa offered to carry out the provisos of the law relating to colonization. Almost all the colonists set out for Sonoma on horseback or in oxcarts; they crossed San Francisco Bay by the Strait of Carquinez in a launch manned by Indians from Mission San Jose, and a small boat.

In Sonoma we were sheltered in the mission quadrangle, the rest of which was occupied by Don Mariano Vallejo, military commander, and his troops.[12] We got very little support from the government for our [f 12] colony, and had to overcome many difficulties before even a small plot of land was under cultivation. We went along in this way, hoping things would get better and the government would make good its promises. But when we least expected it, Vallejo's troops surprised us, took our arms, and arrested the whole colony, ordering us back to Monterey at once. Later we found out that Figueroa had gotten the idea from Vallejo that we were conspiring against the government.

I was a boy of about sixteen, but since my father was one of the principal and most active colonists, I was aware of all that went on, and I am perfectly satisfied there was no such conspiracy [f 13] anywhere but in Vallejo's imagination. The colonists were all too busy trying to clear the small plots the government had granted them. In the evenings Padrés and other leaders gathered at my house to play music, sing and enjoy themselves. They talked about the progress of the colony, but there was never a word of conspiracy nor anything like it, or I would have known it. Perhaps the events in southern California, and the part played by some of the colonists there, caused Figueroa to treat us so badly as a precaution.[13]

After the order of expulsion, most of the group went to Monterey and some stayed at San Jose, Santa Clara, San Juan, etc., everyone obliged to live as best he could without any [f 14] help from the government. The colony was dissolved, the settlement was abandoned and the leaders banished as disruptive elements in the peaceful territory, so it was said.

They were sent off in the frigate *Santa Rosa*: Híjar, Padrés, Captain Verdusco, Doctor Torres, Apalátegui, González, Romero the lawyer, Nicánor Estrada the cavalry captain, Araujo and others.[14]

It has often been said that the Cosmopolitan Company had a private understanding with Vice-President Gómez that when the colony had taken over California the territory would be independent of Mexico. This idea, according to what I have been able to ascertain, occurred to Santa Anna because he mistrusted and feared Gómez as a liberal. Since the colonists were all liberals too, Santa Anna imagined Gómez was trying to set up [f 15] a base of power here for ulterior motives.[15]

The chief opposition to the colony was from the customs administrator, Don Angel Ramírez.[16]

The posthumous publication of Figueroa's version of the dispute as the *Manifesto of General Figueroa*, to my knowledge contains several inaccuracies that ought to be corrected.[17]

The failure of the colony was due firstly to the distrust between Santa Anna and Gómez. Santa Anna's orders to Figueroa were simply to refrain from turning the civil government over to Híjar, with no provision for anyone to carry out the instructions for the establishment of the colony as projected. This occasioned the controversy between [f 16] Híjar and Figueroa —but all disagreements aside, the fact was that the property of the missions was the only actual wealth in California at that time, coveted by the greedy. The communications cited in the *Manifesto* were pure guesswork, disproven by the end results.[18]

The pretended philanthropy towards the mission Indians, to teach them morals, educate them, and assign them the worldly goods belonging to them, was exposed by subsequent events, as all the world is aware.[19] The missions fell into the hands of administrators, most of them the same men who formed the territorial assembly and had constituted themselves saviors of the indigenous peoples and defenders of their interests.[20] The result was complete abandonment of the poor neophytes, encouragement of vice, and neglect of even the scraps of religious education given them in the time of the padres. [f 17] In this way, more than 20,000 workers who would have been useful in developing the country and the farms which at that time were the only resources, all vanished. Most of the administrators were poor when they started, but in no time they were the owners of the most valuable ranches formerly belonging to the missions, with great herds of horses and cattle — and the missions were poor.[21]

Thus I hope to knock down the castle of cards, all unproved theory, erected by General Figueroa and the territorial assembly. Posterity will judge between them by the end results. I don't want to justify or exalt the views and intentions of the directors of the colony, but if their intentions were bad, why did they bring intelligent, educated men with their families when [f 17½] a bunch of hooligans would have been cheaper and more suited to the purpose?

The Mexican government, or rather Santa Anna, broke his promises, abandoned the colonists so far away they could never get home again, where they could subsist only with the greatest difficulty. As an indication of how useful the colonists were to the country even so, when they were scattered, they held government jobs, started

Señor Commandant
Gutierrez and the
cannonball (next page)

industries, and taught school; many prominent native sons owe them what little knowledge and education they have.
[f 18]

[II]

After the colony broke up, my father and other colonists moved to the Amesti Ranch on the Pajaro River and started farming. When the civil governor Colonel Don Mariano Chico arrived at the beginning of 1836, he summoned my father to appoint him administrator of Mission San Miguel. But then Chico left California very abruptly and the appointment did not take effect because my father didn't want it; he returned to Monterey.

I am not sufficiently informed of all the reasons why Sr. Chico left for Mexico. He was an impetuous man; that and his lack of judgment gave him a bad reputation in the country. He was immediately embroiled with the municipal government of Monterey and the whole population as well. When he went, he left Lieutenant Colonel Don Nicolas Gutiérrez in charge, promising to return with troops to enforce his authority; but he never did, and I don't know where [f 19] in Mexico he ended up.[1]

We were in Monterey when the rebellion against Gutiérrez broke out in November of 1836. The ostensible cause of this was a disagreement between Gutiérrez and the deputation. The truth of the matter was that Don Angel Ramírez wanted to run the country and Gutiérrez wouldn't allow it. Gutiérrez was accused of incompetence, misappropriation of public funds, vice, corruption and setting a bad example. All these charges were true, but the main cause was the first reason I cited above.[2] Alvarado and Castro were young men then, and would not have aimed so high if it hadn't been for Ramírez's advice and maneuvers. Alvarado had a position in customs, and Ramírez thought if he were governor, Ramírez would have the real power in the country. [f 20]

Alvarado and Castro headed a movement promptly seconded by nearly all the prominent citizens of the north. They assembled a force of more than two hundred men to march on Monterey. Some were foreigners; the riflemen were commanded by Captain Isaac Graham, the lieutenant was Garner, and though I never saw him act as such, an Englishman named Coppinger served as second in command.[3] This revolutionary army laid siege to Monterey and took the fort which dominated the plaza and the harbor; there were ten or twelve pieces of artillery, some serviceable and some not.

Gutiérrez had previously called up Captain Don Pablo de la Portilla, who had been in the south with a small detachment. Portilla set out in obedience to orders, but he didn't arrive in time. When the rebels took the fort, Gutiérrez fell back to the Presidio [f 21] where they besieged him. A cannon shot hit the roof of his headquarters, making him think the position was indefensible.

The fort was only an earthworks where the guns were mounted, and a little building made of adobe where a few cannonballs were kept, or rather abandoned. It is said that there was only one of the right caliber for the cannon the Californians used, but Gutiérrez surrendered with his staff and was promptly shipped back to Mexico.[4]

Even before this, some of the deputies had met and declared California an independent sovereign state, offering the governorship to Juan Bautista Alvarado.[5]

After this there was a revolution in Los Angeles against the new order of Monterey. Alvarado and [f 22] Castro with troops from the north went down to Santa Barbara to suffocate the uprising. While they were gone, some Mexican residents of Monterey organized a countercoup led by Captain Don Francisco Figueroa and took the fort. The surgeon Don Manuel Alva, Don Florencio Serrano, and several Figueroas took part; I don't remember the names of the rest.

They held the fort some three days during which no reinforcements arrived. My father was at that time in the south, and I was in Monterey, but I stayed out of an affair which which was obviously ridiculous as well as risky.

In about three or four days Captain José María Villavicencio arrived with a few men, and Captain Graham with some riflemen. Graham occupied a hill overlooking the fort, and the rebels had [f 23] to surrender. They were detained a while, very well-treated by Villavicencio, and were eventually freed.

Don Francisco Figueroa moved to Los Angeles where he acquired some property.

The revolution in the south was easily put down by Alvarado and Castro.

The territorial assembly constituted itself a national congress and passed a series of decrees, among them one promoting Don Mariano G. Vallejo to colonel and commander of the national army.[6]

Matters remained at a stalemate, Alvarado's government repudiated by Los Angeles and San Diego, until 1838 when Don Carlos Antonio Carrillo received the appointment of provisional governor by the good offices of his brother Don José Antonio, representative of California in the Mexican Congress. [f 24] The appointment authorized Carrillo to establish the capital wherever he thought best under the circumstances. The government had been inclining to the idea of sending a considerable military force to California, but Don José Antonio pointed out the Californians were loyal only if they had a native son as governor — his brother Carlos enjoyed great prestige, and if he were appointed all the problems would be settled, the country at peace, and the Mexican government well-served.

At the same time, Don José Antonio brought a decree from Congress declaring Los Angeles a city. The document was copied on blue silk with gold lettering — I used to have one, but I lent it to a man and he never returned it.[7]

Governor Carrillo was immediately recognized by the [f 25] town council of Los Angeles and all of California south of Santa Barbara; but in the north he was not accepted as governor, and both Alvarado and Castro, after a lengthy correspondence, declined to obey the central government.

At this time I left Monterey for Los Angeles, where my family had been for over a year. I found Governor Carrillo mustering men to repel the expected attack from the north. My father and the majority of influential men in the south supported Carrillo as legal governor, so I attached myself to the artillery corps as a sergeant. I had never fired a cannon, but there was such confusion it hardly mattered.

When Alvarado and Castro's army was known to be approaching, we decided to retreat to San Diego to organize and make a stand there, because [f 26] it was easier to defend. The cannon was overhauled, and the skeletal Border Company of Baja California under Ensign Macedonio González was called up, which had two field pieces as well.

At this point Captain Tovar arrived, having fled Sonoma due to a political affair. He joined us and was made commander. Now the governor felt he had enough forces to offer battle. We marched out of San Diego towards Los Angeles, and in Las Flores we got word that Alvarado and Castro had already passed through the city. It was decided that we would fortify ourselves in Las Flores and await the enemy.

Las Flores is a ranch, almost exactly halfway between San Diego and Los Angeles, which used to belong to Mission San Luis. There was an adobe house [f 27] with a tile roof for a headquarters and a pole corral to meet an attack. The corral was lined with sacks, harnesses, saddles and whatever else was at hand.[8]

This was the situation when the enemy force of some two hundred men appeared and proposed a parley and surrender to Governor Carrillo, who was with us.

The parley continued. Although Carrillo's men were resolved to fight, he was a pusillanimous coward. On the pretext of avoiding bloodshed, he agreed to all Alvarado's terms and surrendered, after most of us had dispersed, leaving him with only a few friends.[9]

The second day of the agreed-upon negotiations with Tovar, our commander in chief, we artillery soldiers fired on an advancing party of the enemy with cannonball and scattershot. [f 28] We wanted to see if that would precipitate a battle and put an end to our governor's cowardly negotiations. Tovar said we could do as we liked, it looked to him as though the whole thing was going to wind up like a children's game. The governor called us to order and commanded us to hold our fire, because he was responsible for us. That same night we found out he'd arranged the whole surrender to our enemies, so we deserted. Tovar headed for Sonoma with a good many mules and horses. Many of the men from San Diego went home. My father and others, myself included, started for Los Angeles.

Alvarado and Castro received a hero's welcome when they arrived later. The Carrillos, Ignacio Palomares, Narciso Botello, Ignacio del Valle, Andrés Pico and some others were taken prisoner and all sent (except the governor) under guard to [f 29] Sonoma, command of General Vallejo. Some of them caught the pox [translator's note: no distinction between smallpox and chickenpox; as no one died, it was probably the latter] but fortunately there were no fatalities.

Alvarado sent Governor Carrillo to Santa Barbara. Pío Pico was arrested later and also sent to Santa Barbara for some time, but since he was ill, eventually he was allowed to retire to his ranch and attend to his affairs. One of his ranches had been sacked by Indians who had committed murder and other crimes.[10]

In the meantime, Alvarado had sent Don Andrés Castilleros to Mexico to explain the situation to the government. He succeeded so well he returned with an order from the government to Carrillo notifying him that the government had decided to name Alvarado interim civil governor instead and Vallejo as military governor.[11]

In view of all this, Sr. Carrillo recognized Alvarado as governor and promised to hand over the official papers he had [f 30] signed during his term of office.

Castillero also brought the appointment of Captain of the Monterey Presidio for Don José Castro, who had never been even a private soldier and could hardly read and write.

The government also directed the territorial assembly to make up a slate of gubernatorial candidates to choose from and send it to Mexico. This was done, with the name of Juan Bautista Alvarado at the top; in due time he was appointed legal governor.

Castilleros also brought some arms, uniforms and other gear.

It followed that Alvarado and his party thereupon bowed to the legitimate central government of Mexico, headed at that time by General Anastasio Bustamante,

Commandant General M.G. Vallejo
at Sausalito, after Wm. Meyers, 1846

and abandoned their idea of California as an independent sovereign state.

[f 31] There was no longer any excuse for this or any other part of the territory to deny Alvarado's authority.

[III]

The governor began by reforming the territorial system: he divided both Californias into districts and cantons, with a prefect to head each one and a sub-prefect to help him. The town councils were suppressed at the end of 1837, according to the law passed by Congress regarding the internal affairs of the territories; the prefects had authority to carry out those duties, make reports to the central government, and concede land grants.

This law presumed the presence of men with law degrees and notaries to carry out judicial and civil functions, but if there were none to be found in a given area, the justice of the peace could substitute with two witnesses present.

These justices of the peace were appointed to replace the [f 32] mayor and town council, with this difference: the mayor was president and superior court judge, the first justice of the peace was superior court judge with jurisdiction over serious lawsuits and criminal cases, while the second was the lower court judge for preliminary criminal hearings and minor matters.

The jurisdiction of the military over civil matters, or criminal matters beyond mere infractions of military discipline, had ceased long before according to law, though under Victoria commandants continued to excercise an arbitrary control.

Governor Alvarado also established a supreme court of justice in Monterey. He appointed Don Juan Mallarín president [f 33]and as prefects: Don José Tiburcio Castro for the first district and on his death, his son Don José Castro; in the second district of Los Angeles, the lawyer Don Cosmé Peña, former legal assistant; for the third district, from the frontier of Baja California, no one was appointed.[1]

Governor Alvarado secularized now the few missions that weren't secularized by his predecessors. He established a uniform system to run them, with an administrator in charge of each and a superintendent over all; the latter was Mr. William P. Hartnell.

But all these precautions to preserve the missions were in vain, due to the administrators' mismanagement and the corruption of the government itself. They were destroyed at last, [f 34] most of the demoralized neophytes died and the rest went back to villages of wild Indians.

The Secularization Act provided for the distribution of lands and wealth of the missions to the neophytes, who were to live in organized towns. But instead, the huge tracts of land were given away to private individuals, leaving the Indians with nothing to live on and no way to make a living.

The governor made loans from the mission funds which were never paid back. The administrators got most of the benefit, not counting herds of cattle and other property they appropriated because they knew they'd get away with it. These abuses dated from long before the time of Chico, almost from the beginning of the secularization.[2] [f 35] Even some of the padres were guilty. It is a well-known fact that as soon as the old Spanish padres realized that after the independence of Mexico they would lose control of the wealth of the missions, they contracted to slaughter cattle for hides to convert into cash. In this way thousands upon thousands of head of cattle, the wealth of the country, disappeared. This noxious system continued under Alvarado's administrators as well.[3]

I should say, in justice to Sr. Alvarado and Sr. Castro, that while their administration wasted and stole, they did not enrich themselves personally, but handed the goods out to any people or families who asked for them.

A noteworthy occurrence of Alvarado's administration was the rounding up of all undocumented foreigners, [f 36] supposedly because Isaac Graham and other foreigners, Americans, English and Irish, were plotting to overthrow the government and take over the country. At that time (1840), there was a great deal of talk about this plot, but in my opinion it would have failed anyway; there were few foreigners and they could expect no help from the Californians. They just didn't have the necessary elements to succeed. Be that as it may, Governor Alvarado sent a considerable number of them to San Blas in the charge of Don José Castro.[4]

When they got to Tepic, Castro was arrested, apparently on the strength of representations made to the central government by the English and American consuls. He was court-martialed in Mexico City, but thanks to the expert defense counsel General Don [f 37] Manuel Micheltorena, he was acquitted. Micheltorena also used his influence to see that Castro had means to maintain himself during the trial and return to California afterwards.[5]

The foreigners were set at liberty, and the government had to pay them heavy damages. Some returned to California, Graham among them, richer by thousands of pesos, it was said.[6]

In the last two years of the Alvarado administration there was continual discord between Alvarado and General Vallejo with regard to the use of public funds. They constantly reviled each other to the central government, each offering to resign if the matter was not settled. Finally the government took them at their word and decided to send the territory a general with ability and prestige, along with enough military force to back [f 38] up his authority.

The general chosen for this delicate mission was Don Manuel Micheltorena. The government assigned him a battalion of well-disciplined regular troops, but when he presented his orders to General Paredes in Guadalajara, Paredes refused to let him have the battalion. He claimed it was the only force he could count on to maintain order in his district. Some time passed while the government considered the problem, and at last decided to form a new battalion called "The Permanent California Battalion." Paredes then supplied some eight hundred men, most of them convicts and military criminals from the presidio of Chapala. Some of these were sent to San Blas in the charge of real soldiers, although many managed to desert along the way in spite of precautions. Those who [f 39] got to San Blas were quartered on an island outside the port; still, some managed to desert by swimming or on rafts, although several died in the attempt.[7] Micheltorena arrived at San Diego by the end of 1842 with three hundred or so men.

The central government had promised to send him reinforcements and directed the customs house of Mazatlán to honor his drafts to the amount of 30,000 pesos, if I'm not mistaken. A little while later the reinforcements arrived: some fifty men, the same ones who deserted on the way to San Blas.[8]

When Micheltorena reached San Diego, he found only fifty cents in the cash drawer of the customs house and had to beg the inhabitants to feed his troops out of their generosity. He remained there a few days, drilling his troops [f 40] to the point where they could be trusted with a gun.

At this time, Captain Don Santiago Argüello was prefect of the second district. On December 20 of 1842, he appointed me second justice of the peace for the following year.

I remember that while we were preparing for the national holiday, September 16, we got word that Micheltorena had reached San Diego, so we postponed the celebration until he came to Los Angeles.[9] He didn't come until October — of the next year. But he was received with all the pomp and ceremony the resources of the country could afford: the troops formed a passageway in two lines between the parish church where a reserved seat for high mass was waiting for him and the house of Vicente Sánchez (deceased) where Micheltorena was staying, and when the general emerged from the house with his staff, they moved in procession accompanied by the [f 41] officers and the civil authorities of Los Angeles. A salute was fired as soon as he appeared.

After the solemn mass, he made his way to the town square where a decorated platform was set up. From there he made a fairly eloquent speech suitable to the occasion, after which another salute was fired, and the general returned to his house between the files of soldiers.

Both Los Angeles and San Diego received Micheltorena with great cordiality. There was a great banquet at the house where Micheltorena was staying, attended by the local authorities, the officers, and the most prominent citizens of the area.

Don Vicente Sánchez not only lent Micheltorena the house, he arranged to feed [f 42] him, his officers and troops. Other residents did the same in proportion to their resources: Antonio Ignacio Ávila, maternal grandfather of the present district judge the Honorable Ignacio Sepúlveda, Antonio María Lugo, Manuel Domínguez, Tiburcio Tapía, José Sepúlveda (father of Judge Sepúlveda), and various others.

There were bullfights and dancing in the streets later that night; the whole celebration was one of the most impressive that ever took place here.

While Micheltorena was in Los Angeles, living in Julian Williams's house (which afterwards became the Government House under Pío Pico, and today is the St. Charles Hotel on Main Street and some warehouses), Don José María Castañares,

Don Manuel Jimeno Casarici, and Don Francisco Arce came from Governor Alvarado to hand over the civil powers. I believe Alvarado didn't want to do it himself, so he commissioned Jimeno to do it for him.[10]

A few days later, Micheltorena set out [f 43] for Monterey with his troops. In San Fernando he was informed that the American Commodore Jones had taken Monterey and raised the American flag, so he countermarched back to Los Angeles. There he undertook measures to defend the country. But soon after, the news came that Jones had returned the city, saluted the Mexican flag, and was coming to make his apologies to Micheltorena as ex-Governor Alvarado refused to accept them.[11]

In fact, a few days later Commodore Jones's flagship dropped anchor in the harbor at San Pedro. He and a few of his officers came to Los Angeles to hold talks with Micheltorena. They were received with the proper military honors, and matters were arranged to the satisfaction of them both. At the General's particular request, [f 44] I organized a banquet and a ball afterwards for the American officers; some of our officers accompanied them back as far as the Rancho de los Cuervos, and one or two plus myself went aboard the ship.[12]

While Micheltorena stayed in Los Angeles he promoted Sr. Castro to lieutenant-colonel of cavalry and Don Andrés Pico to captain. He then sent Pico to Mazatlán to beg for money, because the remittances he had been promised never came and he was desperate for money to cover the most basic necessities. However, Pico reached Mazatlán in the middle of an epidemic of pox, [f 45] so he didn't stay long, and I don't think he succeeded in getting what he was after.

About this time, with the general's finances so precarious, Sr. Limantour sailed into San Pedro with a small ship. Micheltorena bought his entire cargo and paid with drafts on the Mexican government. I believe this was the beginning of the business relationship between Micheltorena and Limantour, by which Limantour made his great fortune.[13]

As I remember, Micheltorena was still in Los Angeles when he was informed that General Inestra was in Acapulco en route to California with eight hundred men, arms and artillery train, and that General Don Juan Alvarez, for what reason I don't know, impeded the expedition.[14] Finally Micheltorena decided to move on to Monterey, which was a great [f 46] relief to me as justice of the peace.

By this time Argüello was no longer prefect, and Micheltorena had named the

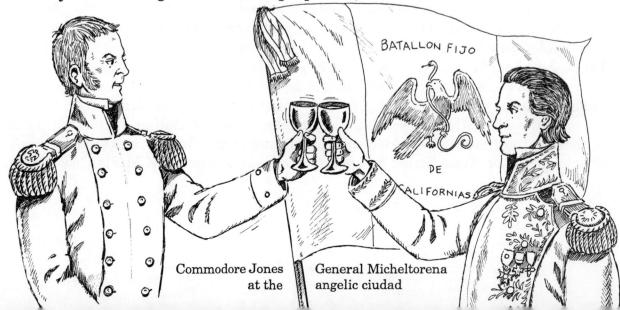

Commodore Jones   General Micheltorena
        at the   angelic ciudad

first justice of the peace, Don Manuel Domínguez, to succeed him. Consequently, I became first justice and superior judge, while Don Rafael Gallardo became second justice.

IV

As superior court judge I was kept busy with constant robberies committed by the Permanent Battalion of California. If I told about all their crimes in detail I'd never be done, so I will only relate a few of the most interesting cases.

One night when there was a ball at Don Vicente Sánchez's house (which is no longer standing), I stationed a guard of twelve soldiers that I had requested from Micheltorena since that was the only way to keep order in those times. There was a great crowd at the dance, in high spirits; most of the principal people of the town were there. We entered on the ground floor. [f 47] The guard was posted next to the bedroom of the lady of the house, who happened to be there. In the room were eight or ten trunks full of the lady's clothes and ornaments. (At that time it was not usual to have wardrobes; the common custom was to keep things in Chinese trunks.)

At about four in the morning Sr. Sánchez came down to his wife's room, a little while after the guard was dismissed. Immediately he noticed that one trunk containing money, jewelry and valuable clothing was missing. He ran back upstairs and informed me. I immediately went down to take appropriate measures. I ordered the streets closed off so no one could leave until dawn.

There was an Indian village nearby, and I had the chiefs keep it closed up too, so I could examine the tracks or traces and find out which direction the trunk had been taken. [f 48] Daylight came, and between the Indians and practiced Californians, the tracks of four of Micheltorena's booted soldiers were discovered. With my men, I followed the trail along an alley between two walled gardens, some eight hundred or a thousand yards, where we found the broken and emptied trunk. The footprints showed they had split up the loot there.

I followed the clearest trail, across an orchard, on what is now Main Street and back then was the only street in that part of the city. I went towards the hills to the west of the populated area, following a creek in the so-called Ditch of the Kings. About halfway up it, I found some of the loot buried in the bank and suspected there was more nearby -- which turned out to be the case. I went on searching and found some more things buried under stones [f 49] in Avila Brook. All I found were clothes, no jewels nor money.

Now it remained for me to determine the culprits. I continued my investigation with the exactitude required by the judicial practice of that time, and discovered the guilty parties.

Micheltorena permitted me to supercede military privilege in making a case against them and presenting it to him. Micheltorena was convinced of their guilt in spite of their experience in defending themselves against criminal charges, and sentenced them to the terrible punishment of lashes and prison.

The leader of the criminals had been in attendance to the general the night of the robbery. They all suffered the lashes and prison term, but they never revealed what had become of the jewels and money. The jewels were well known, because so few people lived in the country [f 50] and fewer still had jewelery. It would have been very difficult to dispose of them without being caught. However, they never did turn up.

A little Payuche Indian girl, who had been raised as a daughter in Sánchez's household, gave the information leading to the capture of the principal thief. Sánchez had bought her from some New Mexicans in exchange for some animals. It should be noted that although it was forbidden by law, at that time the buying of Indians from New Mexico was tolerated in view of the great benefits to the Indians: they were educated and treated as members of the family.

At that time — and before and after it — bands of New Mexicans came with loads of goods to exchange for brood mares, horses and mules. On each trip they took back one or two thousand head. Occasionally they came as thieves and stole immense herds. One of these great [f 51] robberies occurred in the time of General Figueroa, and the last big one I heard of was the work of a Frenchman or Canadian called Charley Fou, who got away with something like two thousand horses and mules between 1844 and 1845, during the war with Micheltorena. Armed men from Los Angeles pursued them, but the thieves outnumbered and outgunned the Angelenos, who returned disappointed.[1]

Another curious episode about Micheltorena's half-breeds was the following:

Don Manuel Requeña sent word to me that some turkeys had been stolen from his poultry yard, and he had been told it was one of the soldiers who took them. An Indian woman described the thief, and when she was taken to the barracks, identified him. But before that, I had asked the officer on duty if a soldier hadn't come in with some domestic fowls. He said no, the only thing any soldier had brought into barracks was a violin. When the thief was identified, [f 52] the officer demanded why he had said it was a violin he had under his arm in a bundle.

The soldier answered, "Sir, that's what we call young turkeys."

Asked what happened to the turkey, he said, "Well, didn't you get some chili from my woman? You ate it up and so did we." He claimed he hadn't stolen the turkey. He had only used a bit of broken needle to tie kernels of corn to a piece of string. For amusement, passing Requeña's house, he had thrown the string and corn over the wall to see if he could catch a crow or something like that. He felt a tug on the line and reeled it in with some difficulty, afraid it would break, and saw he had caught a turkey poult. [f 53]

He decided it was his by right and wrapped it up in his serape. The officer told him that was theft, and he answered that theft was when you took something against the wishes of the owner, but the turkey had come to him of its own free will. This argument did not save him from the whipping the officer commanded.

Those soldiers stole so often I was in perpetual motion. I must say, General

Micheltorena was aware his men were a bad lot and didn't tolerate such behavior. Both as civil governor and military commander, he fully supported whatever measures I wanted to take to preserve order and he dealt out severe punishment to anyone found guilty of a crime.

The general, in private conversations with me, lamented his precarious situation: abandoned by the central government, struggling with the depravity of the troops [f 54] given him. He was aware that their conduct reflected unfavorably on himself in spite of his earnest desire to win the esteem of the Californians by good government.

At the end of 1843, Micheltorena marched north with most of his troops and all of his officers but two or three. During the long stay in Los Angeles, Captain José María Flores (who comes into this history later) married a daughter of Colonel Agustín Vicente Zamorano, and Ensign Garfías married Luisa Ávila.

On the journey to Monterey, Micheltorena had to depend entirely on the charity of private citizens and a few missions that still had the wherewithal. One of his first acts of economy was to suppress the prefectures and subprefectures and the superior courts.

I don't remember what happened in that part of the territory [f 55] during the rest of his term. The same complaints we had here about the Permanent Battalion of California's transgressions became a pretext for the rebellion in Monterey. The principal citizens really wanted to control and benefit from the territorial income in the form of salaries.

Since before the revolt the general had recognized the grave danger of invasion by the Americans, and in consequence he set about organizing militias according to the law. He sent Captain Andrés Pico to Los Angeles with the rank of battalion commander, to work with the civil authorities in forming an auxiliary militia.

The justices of the peace ordered the enrollment of recruits and tried to persuade the citizens to cooperate voluntarily. But there was resistance, particularly from a group headed by Hilario Varela and others, [f 56] even armed defiance; so the militia was never formed.

Things stayed in this sorry state for some time, during which Don Joaquín de la Torre appeared one night with a small band to surprise the guard at the house of the parish priest, which was Lieutenant Medina's temporary headquarters. Although surprised and outnumbered, the guard fought back, losing one man, but wounding de la Torre in the leg. The rebels took the house and arrested the mayor, Don Vicente Sánchez. I think there were other arrests too. That was the beginning of the revolt against Micheltorena in this part of the territory. Shortly afterwards, [f 57] Castro and Alvarado arrived with their band of revolutionaries, pursued by Micheltorena in person.

Alvarado and Castro began organizing their forces here, mustering all the prominent citizens capable of bearing arms. The territorial assembly convened presided over by Don Pío Pico, senior member, and declared it did not recognize the authority of Micheltorena. There were some communiqués previous to the declaration, but I omit them as I assume they must be in the public records.

Micheltorena's army approached, including a rifle company of foreigners and a disciplined force of Indians commanded by Captain John A. Sutter. The rebels turned out to oppose them under Don José Castro and Don Juan Bautista Alvarado, getting to San Buenaventura; and Micheltorena got as far as the Rincon, this side of [f 58] Carpinteria, nine miles from Santa Barbara.

Micheltorena barricaded himself in the Rincon, and the rebels did the same in San Buenaventura for several days.

Sr. Pico, who styled himself governor of the insurgents, appointed a negotiating committee to see if the matter could be settled without the inconvenience of fighting. The committee was made up of Don Vicente Sánchez, Don Juan Wilson and myself. Sánchez and I set out as soon as possible for Micheltorena's camp, where Wilson, who lived in Santa Barbara, would meet us.[2]

Before approaching Micheltorena, we held a meeting at Wilson's house to give him Pico's instructions and those of the insurgent leaders, with whom we had consulted on the way. Having agreed on the main points, we then proceeded [f 59] to the Santa Barbara house where Micheltorena was staying (although his troops were encamped at the Rincon). This was about 8p.m. on the fourth of February, 1845.[3]

We presented our credentials and explained to the general our desire to see if some amicable, honorable and fair resolution could be found for the current difficulties.

Micheltorena answered that his conscience was clear, and he saw no excuse for the uprising at all; in public and private conduct he had demonstrated his affection for the Californians. If he had been unable to do more for them, it was the fault of the central government in Mexico. He had no personal ambitions as governor; he wanted only order and peace in his term, then honorable retirement in recognition of his duty done. He was always ready [f 60] to compromise amicably and make any personal sacrifice in accordance with the law and justice.

We were to inform the insurgents they had proceeded illegally up to this point. If they presented their claim through the proper channels he would listen, and if it were just, he would concede, even to resigning the governorship. In addition, he would not proceed against any of the insurgents, but let them present their case in the full enjoyment of their legal rights.

Since Wilson was not well, and Sánchez was somewhat tired, they commissioned me to take the general's reply to San Buenaventura. I set out at 1am and got to Castro and Alvarado's camp at dawn with the message.[4]

[f 61] Alvarado reacted first. He said Micheltorena had ignored the authority of the territorial assembly, that he was obliged to accept the reconciliation which the legally constituted body offered to settle the current unrest, and that he had refused all amicable solutions. Therefore I was to tell the general that he must resign the governorship, on honorable terms to be arranged. Castro approved everything he said.

I returned to Santa Barbara immediately and acquainted my colleagues with the reply, and we all went back to Micheltorena.

The general said he would answer the message, although he considered it a waste of time since there was no possibility of an agreement.

I went to rest a little in Santa Barbara. While I was asleep, Wilson and Sánchez tried to convince Micheltorena to accept the terms, or at least make a counteroffer which they would immediately communicate to the other side. Then they went to San Buenaventura with no more results than I had gotten: neither side would budge.

Back in Santa Barbara, Micheltorena expressed his appreciation to all three of us for trying to keep the peace, although he was sorry we had not been successful. He also wished, if it were necessary for him to leave the country, to do so in a manner compatible with his dignity.[5]

Later the same day he told me privately that he had sufficient force to resist the rebellion [f 63] and possibly crush it, but his position was critical: the government failed to support him, he had no confidence in his troops, the Californians considered him their enemy, an American invasion was inevitable, and he didn't want it all to explode in his face. He considered the present crisis a way out — if not exactly honorable, at least acceptable to the government — and begged me not to worry any more about the

Don José Castro and Don Juan B. Alvarado at San Buenaventura

negotiations because he knew how they would turn out.

I took leave of Micheltorena to return to Los Angeles. Castro and Alvarado detained me at San Buenaventura, but I told them the same thing I told them before: no compromise on either side. And I went back to Los Angeles.

[V]

Micheltorena later advanced against San Buenaventura and a [f 64] few shots were fired.[1] This had little result, except the rebels fell back to El Alamo and found Micheltorena waiting for them. There was more shooting. Then at Rancho Cahuenga, Micheltorena and Castro came to an agreement (Micheltorena's foreigners having by then deserted).[2] Micheltorena would leave the country with his officers and the Permanent Battalion; a few officers not objectionable to the Californians could stay, like Colonel Segura, Captain José María Flores, the ensigns Garfías and Correa and Sánchez, with a few more. Some soldiers who had deserted Micheltorena were also allowed to stay.

The general marched to San Pedro, where he took ship for Monterey. There he picked up his wife and the rest of his troops and sailed on to the coast of Mexico, to some port.

The truth is, Micheltorena confided in me [f 65] perhaps more than I deserved. As justice of the peace I had to be in continual contact with him, on public and private matters, which gave me the opportunity to learn where he thought California was heading. I can say truly that he had tremendous sympathy with the Californians and believed that with their support he would achieve great progress. He found it incredible that after all their promises of help and support, the principal citizens could betray him. He even confided that if his appeals to Mexico had the effect he hoped for, he'd be glad to take on the Californians, even if it cost his life.

The antipathy between soldier and civilian in the Republic of Mexico is well-known; also that the soldier considers himself superior because of military privilege. Perhaps the same idea caused some of the [f 66] constant friction between Micheltorena's troops and the civilian population. But the general usually upheld the civil authorities in whatever measures we decided to take to insure the public safety; he seldom made any objection of any kind, although some of his officers took offense.

When he retreated to San Pedro after the agreement of Cahuenga, Don Vicente Sánchez and I guided him to the port. About to embark, he said to me, "Coronel, I'm leaving, as I told you in Santa Barbara. And now I tell you without the shadow of a doubt, Mexico will lose California. The only valuable memento I have for you is my watch, which I hope will always remind you of our friendship. Tell the Californians I tremble for the future that awaits them."

We embraced. He insisted on presenting me with the watch, and [f 67] then went on board the ship.[3]

After he left, all the firearms and other weapons he had used in the campaign belonging to the territorial government were turned in at Los Angeles.

So at last we see California again governed by her native sons: Pío Pico as acting governor, José Castro as interim military commander.

Castro and Alvarado remained a few days in Los Angeles, then marched their troops back to Monterey.

Sr. Pico appointed Don Manuel Castro prefect of the second district, which included Monterey. Here in the first district the governor himself acted as prefect, so he offered me the position of sub-prefect, which I did not accept. Someone else, whose name I don't remember, was appointed. But I am sure that on the 25th of June of 1846, Don Abel Stearns was sub-prefect of this district.[4]

[f 68] One of the first things Governor Pico did was reestablish municipal government, authorizing the election of mayors and town councils.

As soon as Castro and Alvarado went north, he sent Don Mariano Bonilla to take charge of the government archives in Monterey and bring them to Los Angeles, the newly established capital of the territory. Bonilla did so, and Pico set to work on land claims and applications for land or government positions, even getting into matters that properly belonged to the justices of the peace and the courts.

Shortly afterward, his confirmation as Governor of the Californias arrived.

Pico and Castro had never been on particularly cordial terms.

Among the notable events of Pico's administration was the abortive revolt led by Sérbulo Varela, José Antonio Carrillo and others in Los Angeles. [f 69] I believe Varela managed to escape. Carrillo was taken prisoner and deported, but he had hardly reached Acapulco or Mazatlán before the central government pardoned him, so he returned to Monterey on the same ship. Castro made him a major general and commandant of the military outpost of Santa Clara.[5]

In 1845, or the beginning of 1846, an Irish padre named McNamara came to California from Mexico with a project for establishing an Irish colony. He asked for an enormous land grant. In support of his petition, he alleged that the colony would be an obstacle in the path of American annexation, because Great Britain could be counted on to intervene to protect her subjects. This idea pleased Pío Pico and some of his friends, who were trying to arrange meetings for people to agree that since Mexico had no power to protect us, we should declare ourselves independent under the aegis of Great Britain. But the majority of the inhabitants of California decidedly opposed this, and the invasion was already upon us, [f 70] so these projects were abandoned.[6]

During Pico's administration, Don José María Híjar was here, the same Híjar who had come as director of the colony in 1834. It was said he came as an envoy from the central government, but I've forgotten what for, if I ever knew. He stayed in the house of Don Abel Stearns, where Don Juan Bandini and his family lived. When Híjar fell gravely ill, Bandini and his family provided all the help and comfort necessary, while I and other friends were able to help out from time to time. Finally he died and was buried with full honors. The death occurred at the end of 1845.[7]

In June of 1846 it was officially known that the Bear Flag Party had taken Sonoma, and Commander of the Line of the North, Colonel Don Mariano G. Vallejo, his brother Captain Salvador Vallejo, Lieutenant Colonel Victor [f 71] Prudon and the ex-mayor Jacob R. Leese were all prisoners in Sacramento.[8]

I forgot to mention that on May 13 of 1846, the territorial assembly decreed that all the towns must elect representatives to decide how to meet the foreign invasion and how to raise money, because the assembly had no resources to draw on at all. On the 30th of May I was elected to meet with the assembly June 15 in Santa Barbara. But as I was about to set out, word came that the meeting of the General Congress of the United Towns of California (as the proposed body was to have been called) would not take place. I suppose the cancellation was due to the opposition of the northerners, although they had been informed well ahead of time.

One of the most notable actions taken by Pico's administration was selling off the missions [f 72] to pay troops to fight the U.S., since it was believed war was imminent between the U.S. and Mexico. However, very little was gained, because the missions were already mortgaged, and with few exceptions, the creditors took them over for a fraction of their real worth.

Mexican colonial law forbade the sale of national property *unless* a foreign invasion threatened; the assembly and Governor Pico utilized this clause, as appears in great detail in government archives.

Another notable action of Pico's admininistration [f 73] was the organization of a militia of more than a hundred men to march north, opposing Castro's force coming south. Communications were very bad, and Pico believed Castro was coming to unseat him; he did not know that Sonoma was held by foreign soldiers of fortune and Monterey by Commodore Sloat, and Castro was falling back looking for resources and reinforcements.[9] The two leaders met at Rancho Santa Margarita between San Luis Obispo and San Miguel, and thanks to the good offices of Don Manuel Castro, they reached an understanding. They embraced each other, promising to cooperate for the defense of the country, and both armies came to Los Angeles.

While the governor was gone, we organized a civil defense force. I was appointed [f 74] one of the captains. We had about one hundred or more men by the time Castro arrived, and at first he wanted us under his command, but we objected that the law clearly stated that the civil militias had to be under the command of the civil governor. So Castro's troops camped in the main square, and we took the courthouse on the same square.

When Pico arrived with his force, Castro again demanded to have all the forces under his command. The dispute wound up in Major General José Antonio Carrillo's house, and there must have been trouble settling it, because we in our barracks and Castro's army in theirs were on military alert almost all day. Towards afternoon Governor Pico came out [f 75] with Castro, Carrillo and Alvarado. They all came to our barracks and told us everything was straightened out, the Los Angeles militia would fight under Don José Castro as commander in chief.

Castro was still engaged in organizing the army when the news came that American warships had put into San Pedro, and Frémont was advancing by land with another considerable force. Our northern troops had brought some of the foreign prisoners with them, including Charles Weber.[10] Castro decided he was vastly outnumbered by the forces against him. He opted to disband his army and flee to Mexico by way of Sonora, accompanied by some of the officers from Monterey, on the pretext of returning with reinforcements. He left two cannons buried [f 76] at Cahuenga, and two more elsewhere, but I don't remember where.

In these desperate straits Pico convened the territorial assembly to advise him. At this time the assembly was made up of Don Francisco de la Guerra, Don Mariano Botello [two blank lines follow, indicating the author hoped to remember more names later]. The assembly agreed the country had no hope of resisting the invasion since Castro's departure. The best thing would be for Pico to leave as well, since with neither civil nor military governor at hand the enemy couldn't impose severe terms of surrender on them. It was widely believed the American army would never get as far as Mexico City. Our object was to leave the central government free to act however seemed best, and any measures taken here would be [f 77] subject to the government's approval.

Consequently, Pico went to Sonora by way of Baja California, returning after the armistice in 1848.[11]

[VI]

If I remember correctly, Frémont arrived first with nearly two hundred riflemen and Indians. Shortly after, Commodore Stockton came with a small force that had landed at San Pedro on August 7th. The occupation of Los Angeles took place on the 15th of that month. The Commodore declared a state of siege and put us under martial law, with a series of edicts we were to obey.

Stockton and Frémont converged in Los Angeles for a brief period, at the end of which Stockton went on to harry the rest of the coast and Frémont threw himself into the diversions of the country. He got to know everyone, and to a certain extent adopted the California way of life. He dressed as a *ranchero*, rode horseback with the *rancheros*, and became such good friends with the [f 78] Californians that even the women of the towns treated him with familiarity. He did not neglect relations with the families that considered themselves superior, but many of those were still fervent patriots and not ready to be on such easy terms with Americans.

In my opinion, Frémont deliberately set out to win over the Californians, and succeeded so well that many prominent men declared themselves in favor of the Americans.

When he went north, he left a garrison of forty or fifty men under Captain Gillespie, the district commander. Since martial law was still in effect, Gillespie was effectively the governor. He kept the justices of the peace, but only to carry out the orders he gave them.

[f 79] Peace reigned, and no one dreamed of disturbing it. The country was entirely convinced that our fate depended on whatever the governments of Mexico and the United States might arrange.

However, Captain Gillespie did not fully understand this and dictated a number of very oppressive measures. For example, people could not walk two together down the street, nor gather together in their houses under any pretext. Shops had to close at sundown so no liquor could be sold to anyone without his permission.

He himself tried those accused of light offenses, such as horse stealing or cattle rustling, and passed sentence according to his own whim. He imprisoned Don Francisco Rico on suspicion, leaving him incommunicado in a dark dungeon. [f 80]

From the first, Gillespie had every house searched and confiscated all types of weapons; his oppressive rules made him as popular as a toothache with the Angelenos.

One of these measures was the spark that touched off the revolt of southern California against the Americans. Gillespie levied an arbitrary fine of fifteen pesos, more or less, on Sérbulo Varela for breaking some rule. Varela fled rather than pay the fine. This was all the excuse Gillespie needed to intensify his tyranny. He began persecuting the principal citizens, many of whom took refuge on their ranches.

[f 81]He pursued Sérbulo Varela with such a vengeance that Varela resolved to annoy the American troops. Various prominent persons tried to talk him out of it, pointing out the risk. Varela replied that he would rather die than live as he was doing.

When he was least expected, he rose up with eight or ten men: Agapito Ramírez (a Mexican drummer boy). . . [Three blank lines follow.]

This was the 23rd of September of 1846. Varela took his band to Gillespie's headquarters, where the Hotel St. Charles is now, between Main and Los Angeles Street. It was an adobe with a big walled corral behind it. The house fronted on Main Street and the corral coincided with what is now Los Angeles Street. Varela and his band attacked from this side, some on horseback [f 82] and others on foot. They banged on the door, yelled "Viva México!" several times and beat the drum. For a little while there was no reaction. Then the American troops peered over the wall, which they used as cover, and started firing on the assault party as it retreated. Agapito Ramírez was wounded, I believe in the foot.

Gillespie of course mounted a defense, and Varela retreated to the eastern outskirts of town. The next day Gillespie began taking security measures. One of them was the arrest of influential people such as Captain Don José María Flores. Flores lived with a family north of the town. He was warned of the impending arrest, but not until the squad of Americans was on the way. [f 83] The lady of the house, seeing the danger, hid Flores so ingeniously that the Americans' thorough search missed him. This is how she did it: she made him drape himself in a serape and get down on all fours, and sat on him.

When the Americans were gone, Flores escaped on foot in the direction of the nearest fields. Soon he met a Californian who took him to safety, riding double on his horse. This was the 24th of September.

Gillespie continued to persecute anyone he considered a suspicious character, until all the Californians went to join Varela in his camp on top of the Paredón Blanco.

All told there were some three hundred men there, or more.[1]

[f 84] The next step was to organize them. Varela appointed several officers that same day of September 24th, including Captain José María Flores as commander in chief.

I was one of those persecuted by Gillespie. I had already left town, in view of the way matters were going, and only visited my home at night. The last night I was there my family warned me that Gillespie's black servant boy had been by the house that afternoon and told my mother in the greatest secrecy that the order was out to arrest me that very night, as well as Leonardo Cota and some others. As soon as I heard this news, I got out a pair of pistols and a sword I had hidden and immediately mounted my horse. I went to a farm, the one I still own and live on.[2]

When I was about two hours on my way, about 11p.m., they entered and [f 85] searched my parents' house. Shortly after, my father sent me a note via our Indian cook, telling me what had occurred and warning me to be on my guard. I left my horse saddled and took other precautions. The next day an Indian servant of mine came running to the farm with the news that armed Americans were on the next farm. I mounted and rode a short distance away where I could see the movements of the Americans. They went to the farmhouse, searched it and a couple of fields; not finding me, they crossed to Ignacio Machado's farm and searched the house there. Still not finding what they were looking for, they went back to town.

The Californian army was organized, although short of guns, and it was suggested to Gillespie that he turn over the town. But before that, we heard from Sra. [f 86] Clara Cota de Reyes and her daughter Inocencia Reyes that they had an old cannon made to fire stone shot buried on their farm. The gun was immediately recovered and mounted on the bed of a cart, tied with rawhide thongs.

A powder keg, not very full, was also obtained at this time. Some cartridges were made for the little cannon and a few old cannonballs were collected around San Gabriel and other places.

What weapons we had besides the little cannon were a few pistols, lariats and knives, and an old flintlock rifle or two.

Gillespie's answer was for us to disarm -- if we didn't, he would be forced to act as the circumstances dictated. Three or four days passed in which we sent verbal messages back and forth. Gillespie meanwhile fortified the highest hill opposite the Pico House,[3] as well as his headquarters and [f 87] Alexander Bell's two-story house on the corner of Los Angeles Street and Aliso. He covered the top-story balconies with planks, made loopholes to fire through, and left a small garrison there.

During this period we heard that a body of foreigners had been organized under Don Benito Wilson. It included John J. Warner, Julian Williams, the three Callahan brothers, David Alexander, Roubidru[4] — I don't remember any more names, but there were no more than forty men. In view of this news, Flores sent about forty men under Ramón Carrillo, Sérbulo Varela and Diego Sepúlveda to reinforce José del Cármen Lugo. He was watching the foreigners, who were concentrated on the Rancho del Chino, property of Julian Williams. Williams was Lugo's brother-in-law. (Actually, I think his first name was Isaac, but he was known as Don Julian.)

I found out from those who were present how Lugo and Carrillo's men surrounded the ranch and called on the enemy to surrender. [f 88] Wilson, the leader, said that he would answer after lunch. But when the foreigners realized how serious their situation was, they shut the main door of the house and spread out to cover all the doors and windows.

The house on the Rancho del Chino is on a flat, constructed of adobe with a tarred roof. It was built in a square, and all the rooms had outside windows with iron grillwork. The main door was closed and barred securely. There was a ditch around it, and a fence made of sheets of tin lashed with rawhide.

The Californians decided to set fire to the house on a mounted charge. At the signal, they all galloped up and threw a bundle of flaming grass wrapped in a sheet onto the roof. They then fell back against the walls to escape the shots from inside coming through the windows and doors, and at the same time preventing the defenders from getting out.

Some shots were fired before the attack, however, one of which killed Sergeant Carlos Ballesteros. His horse jumped the fence but fell at the ditch, and a bullet [f 89] from a front window hit him.

The house was burning well, and the defenders realized that they had no time to lose. The owner, Julian Williams, showed himself with his three young children, crying out that they were California-born and that innocents shouldn't be sacrificed. The Californians outside yelled for them to surrender, which they did. Lugo took charge of his nephews, and the foreigners were taken prisoner and disarmed. Then the Californians themselves put out the fire.

[f 90] This happened on September 26th.[5] The prisoners were conducted to Los Angeles, where the other Californians were harrying Gillespie. They decided to assault the guardpost, and advanced by a circular route with their one artillery piece.

Gillespie already knew about his friends' defeat at Rancho del Chino and could not hope for help to come quickly. He surrendered on September 30th. As I remember, the terms called for him to retreat with his men to San Pedro, leaving his field artillery behind when he took ship. He also left [f 91] the cannon mounted in the guardpost.

So, accompanied by some of the long-term American residents, Gillespie formed up his garrison and marched to San Pedro where there happened to be a ship. He boarded it with his men, after spiking the guns he was supposed to hand over intact.[6]

During the period when Gillespie was besieged in Los Angeles, he had a herd of eighty or a hundred horses, which at night were kept in the patio of the house that served as his headquarters. By day they were taken to water at a nearby stream, and fed stored hay and grain. Ramón Carrillo and Higuera, the blond one, and maybe another man, decided to steal the horses. At all times one of them paraded the Mexican flag up and down, exposing themselves to the enemies' fire from the guardpost, Bell's house, and headquarters. In spite of the risk they ran, not one of them was wounded.

Once when a few [f 92] of the Americans were taking the horses out to water, Carrillo and Higuera waited at a certain place in the Calle de los Negros. When they saw the corral of headquarters open, they galloped out of their hiding place swinging lariats and stampeded the herd. Many shots were fired, but luckily none hit them, and they got away with most of the horses.

A similar episode preceded this one: a dozen men on horseback came out of headquarters with rifles across the saddlebows. They went south on Main Street, perhaps intending to reconnoiter the ground. About a mile on, they came to a field of corn ready to harvest. In the middle of it were two young Californians eating watermelon. They were lookouts, armed with old flintlock rifles from when the territory belonged to the King of Spain. Seeing [f 93] the party of foreigners coming towards them, they decided to give them a good scare. The boys' names were Valdés and Ibarra. They threw away the watermelon and got ready. When the party was close enough they shouted, "To arms, boys!"

Since the corn was tall and dry, and the boys galloped through the middle of it, I suppose the foreigners thought there must be a considerable force hidden in it. They ran like rabbits, in complete disarray, the young Californians enthusiastically in pursuit. One of them tried to shoot a straggler he caught up with, but his shotgun misfired, so he clubbed the man with the stock and brought him down. The other youth tried to catch another, but all the Americans took refuge [f 94] behind an adobe wall. They dismounted and fired a few shots.

The first boy dismounted to look over the fallen man and to take his arms and possessions, but found himself under fire. He quickly remounted, taking a revolver and rifle, and both boys ran. The Americans came out and picked up their comrade. It was said afterwards that he died, but I don't know if that was true or not.

However, from then on the Americans didn't dare go out on horseback.

Viva México!

[VII]

At about this time a detachment of Americans issued from the barracks and went south between farms to Ignacio Machado's land. They halted at the fence. About three hundred yards or more away stood a small house on the flat, where the blond Higuera's brother lived. The Americans advanced on the house and [f 95] surprised the family, taking Higuera prisoner. About eight hundred yards in front of the house was a willow thicket. Blond Higuera, who had got out of the house shortly before, witnessed the arrest of his brother. Without the Americans seeing him, he took cover by a fence near where they had to pass with their prisoner. When he judged it was the right moment, he charged with his pistol and lariat, yelling. The Americans abandoned the prisoner and fled for cover. Blond Higuera picked up his brother, threw him over the horse's croup, and galloped away. The Americans fired after them, but both Higueras escaped unharmed.

When the Californians were again in control of Los Angeles, they began seriously to organize the militia and lay in ammunition and provisions.

There were three half-squadrons of cavalry made up of [f 96] some four hundred local men commanded by the mayor, Don Andrés Pico, Don Manuel Garfías and Don José Antonio Carrillo. Each squadron had a nickname: the Greyhounds, the Spiders, the Tatterdemalions.

Francisco Rico and the other prisoners who had been released joined the forces. As always, there was the same distrust of the leaders.

I was put in charge of ordnance. We mounted two of the field pieces Gillespie left, the only usable ones. Since we were short of guns, we decided to arm the cavalry with lances. The order was sent to Mission San Fernando and other smithies to forge lance heads out of barrel hoops or whatever scrap metal they could find. The shafts were laurel or ash cut in the sierras. At long last, the cavalry had four hundred lances, which were the principal weapons we had.

A council of war decided to take San Diego and Santa Barbara, both held [f 97] by the Americans. Don Andrés Pico was commander of the force sent to San Diego, Don Manuel García was to march on Santa Barbara, and about a hundred men on active service stayed in Los Angeles. The rest were on their ranches but were ready to come at once if called on.

A few of the prisoners taken at the Rancho del Chino were exchanged for Californians in enemy hands; the rest were paroled on condition that they not to take arms against the country.

News came that Santa Barbara was retaken by our forces. San Diego was taken also, if I remember correctly, but promptly reoccupied by the enemy.

While our forces were thus engaged, we heard an American warship had dropped anchor in San Pedro Harbor on October 6th, with an expeditionary force. At almost the same moment, we found out [f 98] they had landed the 7th and were advancing on Los

Angeles. We took immediate action to defend ourselves. Don José Antonio Carrillo, with sixty men armed with lances, three old rifles and a pistol or two, and Sra. Cota de Reyes's little cannon marched out to meet them.

The expeditionary force under Captain Mervine met ours at Don Manuel Domínguez's ranch. The Americans occupied the ranch house, and the Californians surrounded it late in the afternoon. During the night they beat 'to arms' on the drum here and there, keeping the enemy in a state of continual movement and shooting. They were also reinforced by Commandant José Flores and thirty or forty men. In the morning, the American army, composed of soldiers, sailors, and those resident Americans who had left with Gillespie, [f 99] marched out with the soldiers in four files, and the horsemen as outriders.

The California cavalry fanned out widely to stop them, with the little cannon in the middle of the road. Two men on horseback manipulated it with their lariats; four gunners served it, Macario Rivera, Jose Ignacio Aguilar, Agapito Ramírez and one man whose name I don't remember.

As soon as the Americans left the ranch house on the Camino Real for Los Angeles, they kept up a heavy fire on the Californians. The little cannon waited until they were in range and fired its first shot which consisted of bad gunpowder some Sonomans in San Gabriel had made out of charcoal and saltpeter mud from Coyote Ranch and some [f 100] smallshot of the wrong caliber. Naturally it didn't reach the enemy, who advanced with catcalls and jeers.

The gunners leaped onto the gun carriage and the horsemen pulled it to a new position, where it was loaded and fired, again to no effect. This went on until they reached a place called La Zanja, near the Rancho de los Cuervos.[1] The gunner José María Aguilar asked for the best powder available and the right caliber shot to load the cannon. He waited until the Americans advanced within range, confident the little cannon could do no harm. But when Aguilar was about to fire, he discovered he didn't have a light. There were a few embers in the no-man's-land between the combatants, so a Californian (I seem to recall his name [f 101] was Pedro Romero) galloped like the wind to the fire, scooped up a live ember while still in his saddle, and galloped back to our line in a hail of bullets.

One of the gunners touched off the cannon with deadly aim, mortally wounding the American flag officer and blowing a hole in the enemy ranks. They halted; our gunners fired again, causing more damage. Then the Americans picked up their dead and wounded, and retreated, abandoning their gear along the line of march. The Californians followed at a distance, retrieving it.

At this moment I arrived with six men, and Carrillo ordered me to return to Los Angeles to inform Flores, which [f 102] I did. The Americans retreated back to the Domínguez ranch house, loaded their dead and wounded in a cart, and started back towards San Pedro.

The Californians tried to cut them off by setting fire to the chaparral along the way and harrying them to see if they would take the Los Maganos route, where they'd be forced to surrender from exhaustion. It was a very hot day. But it didn't work, because the chaparral wouldn't burn, so Carrillo called the men back. He said nothing was to be attempted without his express order, that enough had been accomplished forcing the enemy to retreat, and anyway there were only a couple of shots left for the cannon; so what if the enemy reformed and marched on Los Angeles again? There would be nothing to stop them.

The Americans, with an eye out for the pursuing [f 103] Californians, boarded their ship. It was said they buried their casualties on a little island in the harbor, formerly the Morro de San Pedro, now called the Isle of the Dead.

The Californians returned in triumph to Los Angeles with the captured enemy flags and presented them to the commander in chief. The action at Domínguez's ranch took place on Oct. 8th. On the 29th of the month, the assembly met and elected José María Flores civil governor and military commander.

Defensive measures were still needed. Supplies were low, and Stearns's and Temple's stores were exhausted. An Englishman named Don Enrique Dalton, who had been a businessman in Lima before establishing his trade in California, was married to a sister of Flores's wife. He happened to have in his warehouse such Mexican goods as serapes, breeches, jackets, boots and shoes, and so forth. Flores appealed to him, and he put his entire stock at the disposition of the militia. His help was crucial. Flores gave him IOUs on the Mexican government, some of which are still waiting to be paid.

[f 104: in the left margin] After October 8th, the American force anchored at San Pedro was reinforced by Commodore Stockton. He landed some eight hundred men on November 21st, but as a detachment of Californians was operating in the area, he re-embarked his troops and sailed for San Diego.

[beginning of folio] Don Andrés Pico's militia was at that time operating near San Diego, where Commodore Stockton had his base.

By now we had no materials of war left, neither small arms nor artillery. Therefore I was sent to Mexico by way of Sonora to see if I could convince the commandant there to send us some help. I had dispatches for the commandant and for the central government, and they gave me the captured American flag to take to Mexico City.

I made my preparations for the journey rounding up a hundred saddle and pack animals, mostly mules. With two soldiers and three of my own servants, I left Los Angeles. When I reached Agua Caliente, J.J. Warner's ranch, I was told a detachment of Americans had left San Diego to pursue me. They had been informed by [f 105] Michael Pryor, one of the American prisoners. The prisoners kept an eye on all of our movements and were able to communicate with their countrymen, all because Don José Antonio Carrillo coddled them.

I didn't believe the news, but proceeded warily in any case. I arrived without incident at the near side of the Paso de los Algodones on the Colorado River. I camped there and met two Indians who told me there were many Americans on the other side of the river. I sent the Sonoran Felipe Castillo, who served as my guide, to see if it was true. He came back the next day saying he hadn't seen the troops, but was told they were there. There was also a party of Sonorans camped across the river, with a herd of horses [f 106] stolen from the California militia —the Sonorans had been assigned to guard the horses and had run away with them. They were alarmed to hear of my presence, because they thought I was pursuing them; they told Castillo I had better not try to cross at the ford.

Castillo knew the men only too well, and advised me to wait for a better opportunity. That same day, Chief Charagüe of the Yuma Indian village sent messengers to warn me of many Americans approaching. Since fords are very exposed places in that region, it seemed wise to withdraw to a protected spot where I could observe when the American army crossed. I sent the dispatches and flag to Mexico with Don Felipe Castillo.

[f 107] I did so, taking scouts and my horses into the sierra between Aguanga and San Felipe. I myself observed the enemy's movements. I sent word to the commander in chief and remained where I was to await orders. He replied that I was to stay there, in case it should be possible to send his American prisoners to Mexico. So I stayed. But I knew the Indians well, and I saw they were getting restless, wanting to go over to the Americans. This had me so anxious I decided to look for a more secure place. All this was at the end of November.

In Aguanga there were some families on the verge of leaving for Sonora. It was already arranged between my father and Agustín Olvera that they would keep in touch with me. For this reason I came down out of the sierra about 11p.m. to Aguanga, where I had a couple of scouts watching General Kearny's army.[2] There was [f 108] a full moon. The lady who was in the tent invited me to supper. I asked if any of my scouts had come in, or if there was a letter for me, and she said no. This was alarming, because the scouts had orders for one of them to report at that hour. I supposed there had been some mistake, and decided to wait at the tent. It was very cold, and I was wet through. The lady and one of my men made a fire so I could warm up and dry myself. I took off my shoes to dry them faster and warm my feet, and hung my jacket and serape to dry. This was December 3, 1846. I hadn't been waiting long by the fire, when around midnight I heard hoofbeats. I put my ear to the ground and confirmed that a party of horsemen approached. I stood back from the fire to see who was coming, and in the moonlight I saw [f 109] the gleam of weapons. Fortunately the woods were nearby, and I hastened to hide before the horsemen rode up and surrounded the tent I had just exited as well as the two others occupied by Francisco García el Zorillo and the other Sonorans.

I climbed a tall cottonwood from which I could see the enemy's movements. I waited, thinking they'd leave so I could retrieve my clothes, because I was in shirtsleeves and barefooted. The Americans arrested everyone they found, including my servant Vicente Romero. They took my horse and arms, my saddlebags and papers. Then I saw them head for the nearby village of an Indian chief named Andrés.

I supposed they were going to stir up the Indians to hunt me in the woods. My position seemed very dangerous, so I fled on foot. From what I had seen, it looked as though the one who acted as interpreter or guide of my pursuit was a [f 110] black named Fisher. He had lived in the country for many years and had worked for me. He was an old man, a carpenter. I also noticed that they took my servant and two Sonorans with them on horseback, presumably to show them where my horses were hidden.

I kept on through thick forest until four or five o'clock in the morning, just before dawn. I came to Chief Alejo's Indian village. It was silent, with only a low monotonous chant from the chief's hut. I showed myself in the doorway. The chief was sitting by a small fire, fletching arrows. His wife and some boys were asleep.

When he saw me, Alejo started up and put his hand on his bow, but I made haste to tell him who I was. He came out of the hut to talk to me privately.

He asked, "What happened to you, little *ñajal*?"

(*Ñajal* is the term these Indians use for [f 111] their masters or acquaintances who are whites.) I told him more or less what the situation was, and asked for a horse to continue my journey.

He said he had none, and no way to get one, but I must go on immediately before his tribe saw me and warned the Americans of my presence. He might be in trouble himself, because all the tribes in the area were up in arms on the American side.

Chief Alejo and the author, see next page.

[VIII]

As we talked we heard a troop of horsemen approaching. Alejo put me in a large barrel, the only possible place to hide. Shortly afterwards, a small party of Americans rode up and asked Alejo if I had gotten this far yet. He said no. They directed him to detain me if I did arrive. Then they went on -- to where, I don't know.

When they were out of sight, Alejo brought me a blanket, a palm hat and a pair of leather sandals, which I put on. He insisted I leave at once, [f 112] promising to lead me to safety high in the sierra of Palos where the Indians were gathering acorns and other food supplies.[1] There might be a horse or two there.

I journeyed with Alejo through thick woods all morning. About noon we started up the sierra, but by the time we were half way the sandal straps rubbed my feet raw and the stones bruised them, so I could walk no farther for the pain. The Indian tore his mantle into strips and wrapped my feet, then put the sandals on again, which brought me some relief.

When we reached the top of the sierra, at about four in the afternoon, we found women and old men busy with their harvest. When they recognized me, they greeted me affectionately and fed me [f 113] *atole* soup made of acorns. But what I most appreciated was an old woman unwrapping my feet and washing them with an infusion of herbs. All pain was gone immediately, and my feet have been tougher ever since.

Chief Alejo meanwhile had gone to find a horse. He returned with a colt bearing Julian Manrique's brand, neither saddled nor bridled, with only a rawhide hackamore and a surcingle. They brought me a sheepskin and I made it do for a saddle, mounting by means of the surcingle. I pulled the blindfold off, and the colt, who was not broken, bucked a few times, but I kept my seat. I went down the sierra at violent speed, and at midnight arrived at Rancho Temecula.[2] There I met one of my family's Indian servants who [f 114] had letters for me. He was with a Sonoran named Parra, who had further dispatches. I borrowed pieces of clothing from both of them and changed horses with the Indian. Then I set off at a furious pace for Los Angeles, changing horses at every stage.

I should mention that while I was in Aguanga, before the Americans came, I heard by word of mouth of certain events in Los Angeles. Later, Don Agustín Olvera wrote me about the same thing. The substance of it was this: Don José Antonio Carrillo, supported by all the northerners as well as the majority from Monterey and a few Angelenos, had surprised the commander in chief in his headquarters, taken him prisoner, and obliged him to surrender his command to Carrillo. (I think this was on December 4th, 1846.) Flores resisted, and the situation was uncertain for several hours. The rest of the army -- that is, the southerners -- thought the coup was naked ambition and risky under the circumstances. They in turn took Carrillo and his henchmen by surprise and handed the command back to Flores. Olvera added that in spite of the above incidents, everything was peaceful for the moment, although the resentments and power struggles were the same as ever.

I joined the army as soon as I returned to Los Angeles.

I forgot to mention that when I got to the sierra of Palos at about eleven or twelve in the morning on December 5th, 1846, I was given an Indian at my disposal to take a message to Don Andrés Pico at San Pascual. I sent the news that the American army had entered the territory by the Colorado River and taken all my mules and horses, [f 116] as well as those of other travelers; let him be careful they didn't take him by surprise. When I arrived at Lake Temascal, the ranch of Don Julian Manrique, at about three or four o'clock the same day, I asked for a messenger to be sent at full speed to Pico with more details. Later I found out that the message was received the evening of December 5th, the night before the battle of San Pascual, but Pico didn't believe it.[3]

I wasn't in the battle, but from various accounts and reports this is what happened.

Don Andrés Pico had adopted San Pascual ranch as his base of operations, as much for its proximity to food supplies as for its distance from enemy headquarters at San Diego, which was kept under observation by a small detachment.[4] General Kearny's army changed the horses they'd ridden from New Mexico for mine, Guillermo Morey's, Francisco Garcia's and others. [f 117] Most of the men rode mules, but the officers took the spirited California horses to ride.

At dawn the morning after my message was received, the Indians warned Pico that many Americans were coming.

The topography of the ranch consists of a creek, the house standing on a small flat and the hills overlooking it. The American army was advancing through a pass in these hills on December 6th of 1846.

Pico was very careless with his army -- most of the men were on foot and the horses were unsaddled. Almost at the same moment the Indians brought the warning, the Americans could be seen. Pico cried "To arms!" and the Californians expertly saddled and mounted with great rapidity. The Americans, observing Pico's position, may have thought it would be easy to take them by surprise; [f 118] they came on rapidly in no particular order, riding half-broken mules and very spirited horses. They were less accustomed than the Californians to managing such animals, and had their hands full just preventing a stampede.

Even though the Californians mounted quickly, they couldn't outrun the enemy. But when they saw that the Americans couldn't use their weapons effectively and control their mounts at the same time, the Californians reined their horses around and charged with their only weapon, the lance. They killed or wounded several Americans. Captain Moore was among those who died -- a brave man who had shown great courage and spirit from the beginning. Both General Kearny and Captain Gillespie were among the wounded.

It was said that when Don Andrés Pico gave the order to advance, some of the Californians took it to mean despoil the fallen Americans, which they did, delaying the action. This allowed [f 119] the Americans to dismount and fire from a little hill nearby. It was not easy to turn their position, so Pico and his officers decided to surround the Americans until they got hungry enough to surrender.

The Americans had a few mules and horses on the hill, and it was said they ate them.

During the standoff Pico had interviews with some of the enemy commanders, but I never found out what was said.

Also during this period, Alejandro Godoy, who was the messenger between the Americans and Kearny's camp, was taken prisoner. Godoy was one of those who came with Frémont from the United States and stayed with him until Frémont returned east. Tomás A. Sánchez took custody of Godoy and kept him at his house in Los Angeles on his own responsibility.

The standoff had lasted [f 120] only a few days when the Americans were relieved by a detachment sent by Commodore Stockton. They joined forces and retreated to San Diego on December 12th.

Shortly afterwards, Commodore Stockton, General Kearny, six or eight hundred men and four pieces of field artillery set out from San Diego for Los Angeles. They had with them some thirty Californians from San Diego, commanded by Don Santiago E. Argüello.

Meanwhile, Don Andrés Pico's men had rejoined the main body under Flores, as did those who had gone to Santa Barbara.

Word also came that Colonel Frémont's army was advancing by land and intended to arrive at Los Angeles at the same time as Kearny.

Flores's staff discussed at length which army ought to be attacked first, [f 121] for any hope of success. A council of war decided to attack Frémont, because he had riflemen and Indians on horseback, and it was thought that the rifle was not effective against cavalry. They decided to let Frémont get down to the flats of San Fernando, where a cavalry charge would meet him. So the larger part of the Californians, myself included as chief of ordnance, started for San Fernando with Don Andrés Pico in command.

Flores and Jose Antonio Carrillo stayed in Los Angeles with a small company of troops.

At that time, Frémont was in the sierra of Santa Susana, where Captain José Carrillo with twenty-five or thirty men kept an eye on his movements.

Pico's army established itself in Mission San Fernando. Some of the men got busy [f 122] making cartridges, while the rest cleaned and sharpened the lances.

Since I was in charge of ordnance, I saw that the paper they were using for cartridges came from the archives of Los Angeles. I made them stop, informed the commander who ordered the undamaged paper collected — but many documents were already destroyed.

At night we were almost all patrolling on horseback, watching the road Frémont was expected to cross.

During this time Kearny and Stockton were still advancing from the south. When they reached this side of Santa Ana, Flores sent an order to Don Andrés Pico to countermarch and engage the enemy. Taking the route through Los Verdugos and Arroyo Seco to the San Gabriel River, without passing through Los Angeles, we met Flores and José Antonio Carrillo [f 123] with their men and a company from Santa Barbara commanded by Ensign Lugo.

We had news that General Kearny was at the Coyote Ranch and supposed he would ford the river at Los Nietos.[5] The flats along the river were somewhat wooded at that time, so it was arranged for the Californians to ambush the enemy. [note added on the back of the folio] (While we were planning the ambush, one of the officers, a Sonoran called Lorenzo Soto, went over to the enemy and told him all about it. We always thought this was the reason the Americans changed their direction of march.) [end of note]

The next day scouts reported that the enemy had left the Coyote Ranch, heading upriver for the ford of Bartolo; so we hastily changed our position.

We had some five hundred cavalry, two field pieces badly mounted, and few firearms. Most of the men were armed with [f 124] lances. The day before I had been appointed officer of the day, and I was one of Flores's aides-de-camp. The others were Tomás Sánchez, Diego Sepúlveda, Francisco Rico, and maybe one other.

The company from Santa Barbara deserted en masse, except for the commander and a couple of men. This was the night of January 7th, 1847.

We prepared for battle at the ford of Bartolo. One wing of the cavalry was Garfías's squadron, the other Pico's. Don José Antonio Carrillo stationed his men a thousand or fifteen hundred yards to the north, with the object — or the excuse — of covering another ford which the enemy troops, or some part of them, might use to take the heights behind us.

Our cannons were gathered on the Paredon, ready to take down to the river flats by the road on the west side.

On January 8th, 1847, Kearny's and Stockton's forces advanced, crossing the ford [f 125] of Bartolo and halting right under our battery. We didn't impede the crossing.

They made a line of defense out of their wagons which were tied together with thick rawhide straps. The troops formed partly inside and partly outside this line, with the artillery between.

I believe the American artillery, directed by Stockton himself, opened fire first. But the bluff protected us, and the shots went over our heads and fell far away. They aimed chiefly at our two guns, so accurately it was difficult to return their fire. We would run out a gun at a propitious moment, fire on the enemy, and snatch the gun back to cover. So the battle went, until [f 126] a shot disabled one of our guns. We fired the remaining one until it too was rendered useless.

I don't know who ordered the bugle to blow "charge." Garfías's squadron attacked with lances and part of Pico's squadron followed.

Francisco Cota, the standard bearer, rode ahead. I think this cavalry evolution frightened the enemy, because they retreated behind the wagons without firing a shot. The Californians rode up close to the wagon square.

General Flores sent one of his aides to José Antonio Carrillo, ordering him to harass the rear guard, but Carrillo was too slow. As they started for the enemy, Diego Sepúlveda shouted "Halt," which [f 127] occasioned much confusion. Some of the men halted, others advanced. The enemy regrouped and subjected us to heavy fire, wounding two men. I thought we were going to take terrible losses, charging head on at a well-barricaded and well-armed foe, but fortune spared us many casualties.

Startled by the firing, the cavalry swerved to the right in disorder. The enemy advanced and occupied our former position.

Our forces that remained on the hill retreated rapidly, moving the cannon to a safe distance out of range of the enemy guns.

We came together that night, two or three miles from the enemy, at the foot of some hills near Alisos Creek. It was decided to confront the enemy again the next day. [f 128] It was very cold. We had no blankets and we didn't dare build a fire, so we suffered a great deal. With scouts keeping watch on the enemy, we spent the night as best we could.

49

IX

Between nine and ten in the morning of January 9th, 1847, the enemy formed a square and marched along the road below the mesa of Felipe Lugo's ranch.[1]

The Californians advanced to meet and surround them at a distance out of range of cannonshot.

The Americans went on and we followed. From time to time they fired at us.

At this point there was an event worth mentioning. Inside the American square were horses and carts. In the last rank, an American was leading a horse with a new saddle, serape and saddlebag. From our side a [f 129] twelve-year-old named Pollorena from Los Angeles broke ranks and galloped down on the enemy heedless of the shots fired at him. The horse pulled back and broke away from the man leading him just as Pollorena came galloping at him. The boy herded the horse away from the column, caught him, and brought him to the Californians. A few shots were fired after him, but he was not hit. It was said afterwards that an American officer had given an order not to kill the boy, only to scare him, because the officer admired such daring.

If my memory serves, the Americans stayed that night on the flats, near Los Angeles, and entered the city on January 10th without meeting resistance. Most of the population left [f 130] for their ranches or for San Gabriel. The Californian army withdrew to Paredon Blanco where most of it disbanded, with each man starting for home. About a hundred men remained with Don Andrés Pico.

I went to San Gabriel to find my family. I believe Flores passed through there with an escort. I went to join him with Enríque Ávila, Leoncio Cota, and others. We caught up with him in San Bernardino on January 11th, following the high road. Flores had taken the low road to Sonora by Rancho del Chino. We all halted on Yucaipa Creek on the 12th, to eat and wait for latecomers.

I knew the Sonoran desert well, and realized it was a risky move, because Flores did not have sufficient provisions. Although my friends and I were well-provisioned and could share in a pinch, [f 131] there wouldn't be much to go around. Many of the Californians gave me to understand that they were sure I would get them out of any trouble, with my knowledge of the country. More than anything, this convinced me not to accompany Flores, although my men said they would follow me anywhere.

I told both my men and Flores's, including Manuel Castro, that if we left this country as an army unit, we'd be put in the Mexican army to fight the United States as soon as we got there, where we'd all be under severe discipline in a strange land. I advised them that we should all turn back and wait on the course of events in California, [f 132] while hiding out in the sierra. If we were pursued, we could still go to Sonora in time.

Forty of us agreed to go back, including the officers Leonardo Cota, Enríque Ávila and Diego Sepúlveda. We started back on the 13th.

Captain Flores was angry with me, but went forward with Manuel Castro,

Garfías, two Soberanes, José Miguel Indar, Francisco Limón and several others. They had great difficulties, and Limón died of thirst in the desert.

We went by the sierra of San Bernardino, walking all night, two or three days after the battle at the ford of San Bartolo. We ran into a storm of snow, rain and wind so violent we couldn't see each other. The soldiers with us were not equipped to withstand such weather [f 133]. They scattered in the brush looking for shelter, covering their backs with their saddleblankets.

We had about a hundred horses and some mules; the wind and rain were so fierce in our faces, we could not make them advance a step. It was decided to stop and wait for the storm to blow itself out, then round up the stragglers. Fearing some of the men might perish, I tried to light a fire both as a signal and for warmth. The cold was intense and we were wet through. I had four men hold a canvas tent over me so the fire would catch.

At that time it was the custom to carry a tinderbox of horn, silver or some other metal, with a cotton wick made by the ladies of the country, flint and steel. I had one, and luckily it had stayed dry. [f 134]. I ripped off a piece of my underwear, which was dry, and took some straw padding out of a mule's harness — we'd already cut a fair amount of twigs and brought them under the canvas. Fortune helped with a lull in the storm, and I got a huge bonfire going. All the stragglers came in, very grateful to me for this great service.

When we were all together I told them these hardships were the beginning of the guerrilla life, or that of any wanderer in the sierras, that I thought it would be the wisest course for each of us to go to our homes and take our chances along with those who had stayed behind, many of whom were more deeply compromised than we were, by reason of their public duties. I proposed we go to the nearest ranch — Cucamonga — and find out [f 135] what had happened while we were gone, what our compatriots and the conquerors were doing.

We broke camp, came down the sierra, and went to Cucamonga. A man named Valdés told us it was all over, but gave no further details. This was on January 14th.

While we were having lunch, a messenger arrived from my father with a letter explaining that I could come home without fear. I should mention that when we decided not to go on to Sonora, I had sent an Indian named Victoriano to inform my parents. The messenger had been looking for me towards San Bernardino, since everyone in Los Angeles knew we were in that area.

We all left Cucamonga together, each one taking the road to his home as we went along. When I arrived in the environs of Los Angeles on January 16th, the Americans were already in the city. The treaty [f 136] between Frémont and Pico was honored,[2] so I went directly to where my family was living on this farm, where I now dictate these memoirs.

Colonel Frémont's battalion entered Los Angeles on January 14, 1847 after the treaty of Cahuenga, so that over a thousand American fighting men were then in the city. Few Angeleno families were left. The Americans broke into some of the houses, but according to what I heard, they only took food and firewood.

On January 18th, the last few dragoons who still remained from Kearny's troop returned to San Diego with him. Commodore Stockton and his sailors left for the port the next day. Frémont's battalion occupied the city until March 17th, when he was relieved by Lieutenant Colonel St. George Cooke with four battalions of Mormons [f 137] and Company C of the First Dragoons led by Colonel Mason, who later became our military governor.

Before the Mormons arrived, construction had begun on a small fort on the hill dominating the city, and the Mormons finished it. This fort consisted of a stockade with trenches and earthworks. It was called Fort Moore, and only lasted about two years.

The civil authorities, that is, the justices of the peace, continued to carry out their duties under Mexican law.

Frémont's battalion went to San Gabriel and was disbanded.

At the end of April 1847 Colonel Jonathan D. Stevenson arrived with two companies of the New York Volunteer Regiment. He was the military governor of the southern district.

In June, the Mormon Battalion was disbanded, having completed its term of service.

February 10th, 1847, was the election of the town council and other municipal authorities [f 138] that hadn't existed since July of 1846. The following were elected: Miguel N. Pryor, Rafael Gallardo, Julian Chávez, and José Antonio Yorva as councilmen; José Vicent Guerrero as trustee; Ignacio Coronel (my father) as secretary.

This council was dissolved by Governor Mason, since it had disagreements with Stevenson.[3] On January 1, Stephen C. Foster took office as mayor, appointed by the military governor, and carried out the office until May 1848.

Frémont came to Los Angeles after the discovery of gold in 1848 and following his trial which took place in the north.[4] He bought cattle from the widow of Leandry, Doña Antonia Cot [sic], and possibly from other people -- to the number of two thousand head, more or less, most of them on credit. He hired Californian cowboys [f 139] to drive the herd north through the tule marshes. After the cattle were sold, the cowboys who returned here complained that Frémont never paid them, and the people he owed had great trouble getting their money from him long afterwards.

Colonel Stevenson was a popular governor, a clever politician, and generous to the poor and powerless. Anyone who went to him in need got flour and other necessities. His term lasted until May 21, 1849, when Los Angeles ceased to be under military jurisdiction.

That same day a new town council was inaugurated: José del Cármen Lugo, mayor; Juan Sepúlveda, vice-mayor; José López, Francisco Ruiz, Francisco O'Campo and Tomás A. Sánchez, councilmen; John Temple, [f 140] trustee; Jesus Guirado, secretary.

As soon as Foster was no longer mayor, Governor Riley appointed him prefect. When this council's term ended, another council served, which functioned from

January 2, 1850, until June 29 of the same year when California entered fully into the present system. For those months the following men served: Abel Stearns, mayor; Ignacio del Valle, vice-mayor; David W. Alexander, Benjamin D. Wilson, José L. Sepúlveda, Manuel Garfías, councilmen; Francisco Figueroa, trustee; Jesús Guirado, secretary. [f 140]

A fair trade? - see page 54.

[X]

When the discovery of gold was first announced and confirmed, several parties set out from here. I went with one of them, a group of about thirty men. I remember Ramón Carrillo, Narciso Botello, Dolóres Sepúlveda, [f 141] José Antonio Machado, Osuña, and several others including a few Sonorans.

We headed north to the town of San Jose and stopped a few days to reprovision. While there, we heard of several places gold had been found. The most interesting was the Dry Placer, and so we headed there in August of 1848. When we reached the San Joaquin River in the Tulare Valley, we met Father José María Suárez del Real, who was a true cowboy and had a fair amount of gold with him. He told us he was coming from the fields of Stanislaus, recently discovered, of very rich ore.[1] We went there, and found the New Mexico Company up from Los Angeles, Americans who had just recently arrived, a few foreigners, and some local Spanish-speaking people from San Jose and nearby settlements.

We camped in the middle of the canyon as del Real had told us. A little before sunset [f 142] four non-mission Indians came into camp carrying bags full of gold, made of animal intestines and averaging at least ten or twelve inches long. I was resting on my saddle, with a couple of ordinary blankets I used as saddle blankets. They were rather worn and dirty, and if I remember correctly, cost about $2 each. One of the Indians took a blanket and held up his sausage of gold, indicating how much he was offering me in exchange. But I had no way of getting another saddle blanket to replace it, so I refused. The Indian raised his offer the same way he made it, indicating with his thumb the amount of gold. I refused again, and again he raised the offer. Then one of my servants said why didn't I let the Indian have the blanket? He would make a saddle pad from straw. I took a tin plate and the Indian poured gold into it. After giving him the blanket, I weighed the gold -- it was seven and a quarter ounces, the first gold I got from the California gold fields.

Immediately another [f 143] Indian made the same offer for the last blanket. I spurned two or three offers before accepting. After handing over the blanket, I weighed the gold and it came to a little over nine ounces.

I had brought a serape from Saltillo for my own use. The Indians began to finger it and make offers for it, putting up four bags of gold which together weighed something like THREE AND A HALF POUNDS [emphasis the author's]. I still refused, since the serape was all I had for protection from the weather. One of my servants, Benito Pérez, sold them a New Mexico serape which had cost him $9 a year before for two pounds three ounces of gold.

This Benito Pérez was experienced in placer mining, and he proposed to follow these Indians to find out where they were getting the gold. If I would give him a companion, he'd follow them. The Indians went around buying more things on the same system, among them an old horse from a man named Valdés for nearly two pounds of gold.

It was dark when the Indians left our camp, and Benito Pérez accompanied by a servant [f 144] of mine followed them. This servant was one of two *Mudos* [Mutsun=Miwok?] Indians with me, called Augustine, raised in my family. He was one of the Indian children the New Mexicans used to capture and exchange in California for horses and other goods. Pérez and Augustine followed the four Indians to the village of Chief Stanislaus, not far distant.[2] Perez made camp on a hill in front of the village and spent the night there, waiting for the Indians to get up. In the morning the same Indians that had visited us left the village, climbed over some high hills and took an easterly direction. Pérez followed them to Mud Creek, keeping out of sight. The Indians took flat wooden stakes and began to dig gold out of the creek bed. Pérez jumped down too. The Indians didn't like it, but Pérez insisted on digging right beside them. With his knife he extracted three ounces of big nuggets. [f 145] Since it was by now pretty late, he took careful note of the place and came back to tell me all about it.

Pérez and I decided to stake a claim immediately, but since I had companions, I thought it would be only fair to let them participate, especially since Pérez told me the place was both rich and extensive. However, the news seemed to circulate by magic, and I realized all my movements were watched. So I arranged for Pérez and my two *Mudo* Indians to go secretly and take possession of the gold field, the richest part. They did, and when I was informed they had achieved the objective, I set out late at night, followed by some of the Spanish-speaking people in camp.

Everyone marked out a claim to work the next morning, October 7th, [f 146] 1848. At dawn, everyone started in. In no time we found gold-bearing deposits, and were well content with the results. I worked all day with my two Indians, and picked up forty-five ounces of big nuggets, not counting finer particles to be washed out later. Dolores Sepúlveda, who was next to me, found a nugget that weighed over twelve ounces, in addition to still more. All in all, more than a hundred people were brilliantly rewarded for their efforts.

The next day I continued, collecting thirty-five ounces of nuggets and leaving the dirt in a pile to sift later.

The third day I panned the pile of dirt and got fifty-seven ounces out of it.

Mud Creek was about a thousand yards long. The head of the valley was where we discovered the gold I have described. From there the valley fell into a narrow ravine and turned south. There was a ledge in the stream about [f 147] two yards wide. A man named Valdés Chapanango, a Californian from Santa Barbara, found where a rock blocked the current in such a way that it collected a deposit of gold. Valdés dug down three feet and found another deposit. He gathered it all in a piece of cloth until no more could be piled on. Then he picked up the cloth by the four corners and went around showing it to us. Fascinated by his discovery, he was satisfied and wanted to leave.

Lorenzo Soto of San Diego, whom I have mentioned elsewhere in these memoirs, was looking for a parcel, and seeing Valdés wasn't working his, offered to buy it. I don't know what he gave for it, but he took possession immediately. I was working mine about [f 148] twenty yards upstream, where I could see him. My claim was whitish-blue mud, as hard as soap, with the gold mixed in. It was hard work panning it, but worth the trouble. Lorenzo Soto worked about eight days on his claim, and from what I saw and what he told me, he got *fifty-two pounds* of gold ($330,000 today). He had dug down to the water table, and at that point he sold his claim to some Machados from San Diego who also found a considerable amount of gold in it.

I left my servants to work my claim and went to inspect the third falls of Mud Creek. With me went one of the Sonorans nicknamed "The Chinese Sharpshooter," a famous prospector. We stopped at a likely spot. He picked out a place high on the bank near where I stood, and I picked the spot where I was. He began digging at once, while I went to get tools and one of my servants. [f 149] "The Chinaman" went on digging; my servant and I did the same. This was at about nine in the morning. At a depth of about four feet, the Sonoran found a deposit of gold beside the rock that separated our claims. He dug out ore with a horn spoon and with his hands, putting it in his wooden pan. He then shook it to get rid of the loose dirt -- what the Sonoran prospectors call "dry cleaning." He kept doing this until four in the afternoon, putting the nuggets into a palm leaf hat. I was observing his good luck, because I had been working much harder and just as long without getting more than six ounces of gold. When the hat was full (it was a big hat), there was still ore in the pan. I suggested he dump the nuggets back in the pan, which was also big. He did, and could barely carry it. He said he was going back to camp, and I asked if I could [f 150] pan for gold on his side. He readily gave permission, and in two hours I extracted seventeen ounces.[3]

"The Chinaman" caused a great uproar in camp with his gold. He went around offering to exchange it for silver, which was in short supply. He had already sold some when I got back, and offered to sell me *pure gold at twenty reales the ounce*. I bought forty-six ounces at that price, because I didn't have enough silver to buy more. Other people bought the rest at more or less the same price. Before "The Chinaman" had sold all the gold, he found out a foreigner had a bottle of *aguardiente*. He went to buy it, offering four or six ounces — the offer was refused. "The Chinaman" kept raising the offer until at last, to get that bottle, he told the foreigner to take all the gold he wanted for it. The man plunged his two hands into the pan and grasped all he could. He put the gold on a tin tray and handed over the bottle, which wasn't even full. I asked him, some time later, [f 151] if he had weighed the gold "The Chinaman" gave him for the *aguardiente*. With a certain indifference he told us all it wasn't much, hardly more than two pounds.

"The Chinaman" used the silver he had exchanged his gold for to set up a game of monte. He spread out a wool blanket on the ground. I must add that he had no more clothing than canvas breeches and a wool shirt, besides the blanket. By ten o'clock that night, or even earlier, he was drunk on the *aguardiente* and didn't have one *real* left — he'd lost it all. The next day he went back to his claim, but during the night many people had exploited it by candlelight, taking out great quantities of gold. When he realized that, he decided what was left wasn't worth the trouble.

Felipe García of Los Angeles took over the claim and got some twenty ounces out of a little puddle he found.

There were so many similar incidents it would take too long [f 152] to tell them all. I left that claim to go back to my previous one and worked it for a month or a few days less.

By the onset of winter, everyone in the Stanislaus area with few exceptions had a good stake of gold and wanted to get back to civilization. Rumor had it that the snowfalls were terrible and made it impossible to bring in supplies. Still, no one left, because there was also a report of thieves on the San Joaquin River.

Don Andrés Pico had brought a party of Sonorans to Stanislaus from Los Angeles and fully equipped them, on condition they pay him back in gold at the going rate. To make sure he got his money, he had them working all in one place under the supervision of a Spaniard named Juan Manso, one of the administrators of San Fernando.[4] When this group announced [f 153] that they were setting out for San Jose, most of the other prospectors went too.

The Californians had all brought extra horses, and they abandoned them to run wild or they got together and paid a high salary for someone to ride herd on them. Even so, many animals strayed, and when it was time to break camp, many men found they had no mounts. There was a lot of confusion as some took other people's, with the excuse of family ties and friendship. The upshot of it was that nearly all of them left on horseback, their own mounts or someone else's.

I had decided to winter there, because my claim was rich enough to work all winter if weather permitted. I was just getting ready to build a house when I received a letter from Don Ramón Carrillo, brought by José Antonio Machado and [f 154] one of the Osuñas. I was invited to try my hand at placer mining in the north, where Carrillo had a very rich claim, and had twenty or more Indians, and plenty of livestock at his disposal. He wanted me to go and take charge of it all on equal shares. The bearers of the letter, both friends of mine, urged me to accept. So my servants and I, Benito Pérez, Dolores Sepúlveda (who was a brother-in-law of Ramón Carrillo's), Osuña and Machado set out north to the place Carrillo had indicated.

[XI]

Before I reached the place on the North River I met with Juan Padilla coming back. He told me Ramón Carrillo had sold his stock, given the Indians to another master, and retired to Sonoma. Disappointed, I resolved to spend the winter in Sacramento or San Jose. When Padilla heard that, he invited me to accompany him to his good ranch with fat stock near Sonoma. [f 155] I could exchange my horses and go right back to the gold fields. I gave in to his entreaties, and we went to Sonoma, arriving mid-December of 1848.[1]

I sent my horses on to the ranch immediately, and began to look for placer mining. I was staying in a house belonging to General Vallejo, next door to the one in which he lived. Owing to our previous acquaintance, he was the first person I looked up when I arrived.

At that time there was a troupe of actors performing in an improvised theater. Vallejo, Padilla and I, and some others decided to attend a performance. Afterwards, Vallejo invited us to the new hotel he had just opened — if I remember correctly, it had belonged to his brother-in-law Jacob P. Leese.[2] It was not far from the theater, on the same side of the street. We entered a big public room with a bar and a [f 156] card table where several Americans and foreigners were playing monte. Others watched.

Juan Padilla and a Sonoran called Carmelo went over to the table to watch too, and were joined by a Californian named José de García Féliz. Dolores Sepúlveda headed for the bar. Vallejo and I went to look over the hotel rooms, then came back to the same public room. Then Vallejo left for his own house, and I stayed with my friends.

I must admit that I was already aware of the critical situation of Juan Padilla in Sonoma. He was accused of atrocities during the Bear Flag invasion against American citizens, his and Ramón Carrillo's prisoners. Some friends had warned me to be careful not to let anything happen to me, although I was [f 157] known and respected by the most decent people in Sonoma.

Therefore, I thought it would be best to get Padilla out of there, reminding him he was in danger. He answered that he just wanted to see what happened with the first hand dealt, in which the newcomers, particularly Carmelo, were interested. I went back to the bar where Sepúlveda was about to light a cigar. At that moment, the gamblers' voices rose. I hadn't finished lighting my cigar when there was a commotion and the lights went out. Someone grabbed me by the arm, shoved me into a room next to the bar and locked the door. Naturally I was alarmed and looked for something to defend myself with if I had to. I found an iron bar and crouched near the door, hearing the tremendous racket of shouts, blows, breaking furniture and so forth. [f 158] Soon after, all was silent. A black man lit a light in the bar, and I opened the door. I don't remember if the person who pushed me into the room locked the door and someone else unlocked it. I came out, and the first thing I saw were several broken chairs and Padilla lying in his own blood on the floor. He was unconscious, with many head injuries and bruises on his face. Sepúlveda was in a corner, behind the counter. The assailants had vanished.

I sent for my servants to take Padilla to his room, which was next to mine. I also sent for a German doctor who knew the injured man. Thanks to the doctor's skill, and my constant care, the patient lived. He was not able to speak for ten or twelve days, or open his eyes for two or three weeks because his whole face was swollen black and blue from the blows. When he could open [f 159] his eyes, the whites were purple. He didn't take solid food for a week, only liquids from a cup with a pouring spout. In a month he recognized people and was conscious, but not in his right mind. He talked wildly and tried to tear the bandages off his head. Someone was required to watch him day and night. My servants and I were the only ones willing to perform this humanitarian service. I tried to get someone to take charge of him, offering to pay whatever they asked so I could return to the gold fields, but found no one to do it. So I had to spend all winter in Sonoma at my own expense.

During Padilla's infirmity, public feeling still ran high against him. On several occasions Americans and others came into the sickroom shouting and making threats. But others, including Americans who esteemed me, persuaded them not to make any violent assaults on [f 160] Padilla while he was under my care. I think that was why he wasn't torn to pieces, and I received no hurt.

Before I went to Sonoma with Padilla, I had heard the accusations against him and Ramón Carrillo. I had also heard there wasn't a word of truth to it. Carrillo and Padilla themselves assured me it was pure calumny, and they could prove it.

When Padilla recovered, about mid-February, I moved to San Jose by way of San Francisco, because at that time transport to San Francisco was difficult. I arrived a day or two before Washington's Birthday, landing on the beach which then reached to what is now Montgomery Street.

San Francisco looked more like an army camp than a city, with more tents than houses. There was a crowd of all nationalities, stricken with gold fever, [f 161] anxious for transport to the gold fields and eager for information from anyone who came from there. I was mobbed as soon as I got off the boat. I gave short answers and managed with difficulty to reach Mr. William Howard's store to rest.

I wanted to know about lodging houses, safe if not comfortable, but that was difficult too. Someone gave me a hint, and going down the street towards the plaza of Yerba Buena (Portsmouth Square today) I met a German, formerly of Colonel Stevenson's regiment, who had gone into business in Los Angeles. He spoke some Spanish by now, and when he heard what I was looking for, he offered to take me to his own house and lodge me in comfort and security.

A young man named Manuel Serrano accompanied me. All three of us went to the [f 162] house, situated on what is now Kearny Street, near Telegraph Hill. The hut —for it was no more than that—was constructed of upright planks. Two rooms below, a dining room between them and a kitchen, with a slat-covered porch above. I didn't much like the look of it, but night had already fallen. I heard a great racket and gunshots, and saw unsavory looking characters wandering around. So I accepted the lodgings at once. To tell the truth, the German did his best to reassure us. I didn't distrust him, because in Los Angeles I had known him for an honest man — but there were cots and beds close together in the downstairs rooms, and bunks against one wall. The German took me up to the porch, where he and a partner of his slept, and fixed up a bed for Serrano and myself. Although it was not very comfortable, it was the best circumstances permitted. We settled in and shortly after went to sleep.

[f 163] About two hours later the German's partner came in, very excited and looking for something — a weapon, I supposed — because there was an argument downstairs. We got up and went to see what it was about. In the street we heard drunken partying, and the argument downstairs rose in volume. I told Serrano we'd better get out of there, but unfortunately the stairs were only a ladder, which had been removed. By now there was a fistfight going on, in spite of the owners' efforts to break it up. I was afraid someone would pull a knife or a gun, but fortunately the wall of bunks fell down with a crash. The porch had a window giving onto the roof of the dining room and kitchen, and Serrano and I escaped in the confusion [f 164] without inquiring further into the matter. We made our way to Mr. Howard's store and banged on the door for them to let us in. They let us spend the rest of the night, although the counters, tables and floor were occupied fully by friends of the house.

The next day I took a small boat to Mission San Jose, because there was no direct route to the town of San Jose, and my business was urgent. I had two or three days in the town and had to leave because the launch, named *The Box*, owned by Pedro Sansivain, was sailing for San Francisco. With some difficulty due to a storm which caught us midway across, we arrived in San Francisco. I stayed a few days more and returned to Sonoma.

I got my animals back and made the necessary preparations to set out for the gold fields on March 2nd, 1849. I was heading for the Stanislaus area, but in Sacramento I met people coming back from there who [f 165] told me it was overrun with all sorts of people, especially Sonorans. My claim, which I had left to a friend, was occupied by William Wolfskill. They also told me the Placer Seco was producing well, so I decided to go there with my servants and four companions.

At the same time as my departure from Sonoma, Juan Padilla left for the north.

A Yankee discussion at Sonoma

[XII]

At the Placer Seco I set to work on a moderately rich claim. There was already a large population of Chileans, Peruvians, Californians and Mexicans, with many Americans, Germans, etc. The camps were separated by nationalities. Everyone, more or less, was profiting by his labor.

But then a rumor got around that all but American citizens were going to be expelled from the gold fields, on the premise that foreigners had no right to exploit them.

One Sunday a written notice appeared in several places, to the effect that non-citizens had twenty-four hours to leave or be thrown out by force. The notice was backed up by a party of armed men.

There were a considerable number of foreigners affected by the notice. They united on a defensible hill in case of attack. The day they were supposed to leave, and for three or four days after, both groups were on armed alert. Nothing but insults, shots, and drinking came of it, and in the end everyone calmed down and got back to work. However, the strong constantly stole from the weak.

A few days afterwards, a Frenchman named Don Augusto and a Spaniard named Luis, acquaintances of mine I had always considered honorable and well-bred men, were arrested. [f 167] Everyone who knew them was of the same opinion and was very surprised at the arrest. Some of the leaders among us met and commissioned me to investigate.

I went to see an American named Richard whom I had known in Los Angeles as a sergeant of cavalry, and requested him to investigate why the men were arrested. He answered at once, they had been accused of robbing an old Irishman of four pounds of gold he had buried. I informed the committee, and without loss of time we got up five pounds of gold to pay for the prisoners' freedom.

I went to the leader, who looked disagreeable and angry. Through an interpreter I made my proposal, adding that the men were of good reputation and had plenty of gold of their own with no reason to steal; I had with me five pounds of gold, [f 168] one more than the old Irishman claimed to have lost. The leader took the gold and said he would present the case to his committee and return in three or four hours.

Before the time elapsed, I observed a great deal of movement of armed men, most of them drunk. Then a cart pulled out, in which our two friends were carried with arms tied behind their backs, guarded by two men in the cart. Many others followed on foot and on horseback. On the cart was clumsily lettered in charcoal a notice that anyone who interfered with the prisoners would meet the same fate. They arrived at an oak tree for the hanging. With the ropes around their necks, the prisoners asked for paper and pen to write to their families and settle their affairs. They got only a blow for asking. The cart lurched forward, and the unfortunates were left hanging.

I was deeply shocked, [f 169] as were many others. Two days later I set out for the northern gold fields.

The reason for the prejudice against anyone of Spanish descent was the preponderance of Sonorans. They were skilled prospectors and got richer quicker. The Californians had learned too, with the advantage of arriving first. The latecomers, burning with the terrible gold fever, might find little or nothing with their efforts; or not enough for their ambition to get rich in a minute. These, I say, couldn't bear to see others' good fortune. Add to the gold fever continuous drinking. Add to that, the fact that a good proportion of them were criminals capable of [f 170] anything, and there was no effective legal authority to protect the rights or the lives of peaceful and honorable men against evildoers. In fact, there was no law at all except might makes right in those times. In self-defense, the decent people had to adopt the principle of an eye for an eye.

I reached the gold fields above the North River (the one that joins the Sacramento past Marysville). While looking for a likely claim, I came to the camp of a Spaniard from Los Angeles. He had set up a small grocery and butcher shop. I camped near him in order to find out where the best places to pan gold were located. In the course of the conversation he gave me to understand that he was satisfied with what he had and was looking for someone to buy his business so he could go back to Los Angeles. It looked like a good deal. We settled for five pounds of gold [f 171] for stock which today wouldn't be worth a hundred dollars. But the value of the location was doing business with a peaceful Indian village close by. The way they did business was to pour a little gold into the palm of one hand and holding it out, pointing with the other hand to whatever they wanted to buy. Even a small quantity of gold was worth at least twice the price of anything for sale, and sometimes four times as much.

This was how they bought meat: on the hanging quarters they indicated what cut they wanted—the shopkeeper capriciously cut whatever piece he thought suitable. If it didn't look like enough, the Indian added more gold to his palm and the shopkeeper more meat, until both parties were satisfied.

I took over the business, bought six beeves at $100 a head, and in a couple of weeks I made [f 172] fourteen pounds of gold. It seemed like a good business, and I decided to expand. Leaving a brother of mine with my servants to run it, I went to Stanislaus to buy a small string of mules, planning to load them with goods in Sacramento.

Stanislaus wasn't the same place it had been when I left months before. It was full of brush shelters and tents. There was a great deal of gambling, in which gold was treated not like the most precious metal, but something easy to come by. I saw men who didn't look worth a *peseta* stake bags of gold on a single card. Each of those bags today would ensure the happiness of a whole family, insofar as happiness requires money.

The men who lost such sums were entirely indifferent [f 173] and worked the next day just the same. They didn't mind paying fabulous prices for whatever they happened to need.

On the way to Stanislaus, about two miles below Sutter's Mill, I stopped for the night. I hadn't been there long when a party of foreigners of various nationalities arrived. Among them were Sisto Berreyesa and one Molina, the first Sonorans who had come to California. This party brought a number of Indians as prisoners, forty men, ten or twelve women and five or six children of both sexes. They camped near me.

To prevent any of the Indians from escaping they made the men lie on their backs in a circle, with their feet towards the center, which were then tied. Guards watched them, hardly allowing them to move at all. The Indians were naked -- it was very cold -- and no fire was allowed them. The [f 174] women and children had a small fire which also served for the guards. The head of this party came up to me and asked me to help guard the Indians as he had to go on an expedition to a nearby place. I excused myself saying I had to leave very early in the morning.

Sisto Berreyesa told me that the "expedition" was a punitive raid on an Indian village on the American River because two Americans had turned up dead, and the Indians were blamed. In the dark before dawn the party set off, leaving Molina and two others to guard the prisoners. Out of curiosity I saddled my horse and followed them at a distance, careful not to be seen. At first light they surrounded the village and opened fire.

What followed was a scene of utter horror. Out came old men, women, [f 175] children -- everyone -- some with bows and some with nothing, running in every direction, even throwing themselves into the river. They were all rounded up and shot down. I couldn't go on watching the horrible massacre so I withdrew to my camp. This occurred about the end of March, 1849.

I got ready to begin my day's journey at once. In a little while some of the foreigners came back to let the prisoners get up from the ground. I gathered that they were to be put with others taken alive from the village. The party went on to Sutter's Mill.

I traveled on to the Cosumnes River, where some twenty armed men caught up to us, passed, and turned off the road to the east. We went on. When we came to the open range country we made for a ranch which I believe belonged to Mr. Hicks. He had great fields of wheat and an Indian village for labor. As we rode up to the house, we saw several Indians fleeing in different directions, and the men who had passed us earlier [f 176] hunting them down and killing the ones they caught.

So as not to witness this spectacle any further I abruptly changed direction and hurried away. Later I was told the atrocity reached a point where the Indians tried to take refuge in Mr. Hicks's house. The assassins did not even respect the privacy of the house. They entered and dragged the Indians out to murder them.

The condition of these wretches at that time was such that killing an Indian in cold blood was the same as shooting a rabbit. This infamy came to the attention of the military governor, who came personally to put an end to it.

I got to Sacramento with my string of mules, loaded them, and set out north for my store. But about fifteen miles from Sutter's Mill, I met my brother I'd left in charge, with the servants and several others of Spanish blood, fleeing on foot. They told me [f 177] a party of foreign gunmen had run them off, without letting them have so much as a mount.

I returned to the Mill, where there was a little settlement. I knew some people who lived there, and I hoped I could sell my goods and abandon the gold fields. I sold everything and almost all the mules, at such low prices I lost two thirds of my investment. Those people took advantage of my predicament.

Then Juan Manso arrived with a few Sonorans, still under Pico's command. Ramón Carrillo also arrived with a few friends from Sonoma.

I was faced with the choice of going on or retreating as I had planned. A man named Fisher, a shopkeeper of Sutter's Mill and an old acquaintance from Los Angeles, came to us with other merchants and tried to persuade us that most of the people didn't approve of such [f 178] outrages, that these acts must be the work of a small group of outlaws. They insisted it was public knowledge and well understood that Californians were considered equal to other Americans. We would be given a credential identifying us as citizens meriting all respect, signed by the principal inhabitants of Sutter's Mill. I still didn't want to go back to the gold fields, but I gave in to the others.

A vile affair

[XIII]

Now a party of forty, we prospected up the American River and its tributaries — it was Benito Pérez who found gold. The next day I went with him to examine carefully his discovery. I was sure there was enough gold to keep the whole party busy for two or three weeks.

We settled there, [f 179] and it looked like this: an island about two thousand yards long and more than two hundred wide, forming an angle opposite a ravine where the Vacas -- New Mexicans who lived in Sonoma -- had found rich ore.

Pérez and I decided after our inspection that the island was formed by buried rock that didn't show on the surface. The gold had collected around the rock of the whole island in a two-foot-wide strip of earth. The depth varied from three to ten feet, and it was necessary to take out a lot of rock to get to the vein. There was no gold in any other part of the island, although we looked for it.

I was elected captain of the group in order to lay down some ground rules to ensure our safety. If any stranger [f 180] happened by, he was to be told nothing. If the claim was being worked at the moment, work must be suspended and everyone must pretend to do something else. No one was to go to Sutter's Mill. If supplies were needed, a very discreet person would be assigned to get them.

In Ramón Carrillo's party there was an Irishman, long established in the country — a good fellow, but fond of his whiskey. I mentioned to Carrillo my worry that he would let out the secret. Carrillo assured me he was entirely trustworthy.

When we were settled in, Carrillo went to Sonoma, and we got to work. The first claim, some ten yards long by three wide, was for my servants and myself; the second, for Manuel Serrano and his brothers; the third, Dolores Sepúlveda; the fourth, José [f 181] de García Féliz; the fifth, the Irishman for Carrillo's party; the last three or four went to other Californians and Sonorans.

On Saturday, after the week's work, we washed the gold-bearing gravel we'd collected. We were all pretty satisfied with the results, as good as we had hoped.

During the week while we were digging every day, people came to inspect the area and ask us questions. We always answered that we were prospecting and hadn't yet found anything. Féliz and the Irishman had gotten over two pounds of gold between them in the first week. My three servants and I had over seven pounds.

But Saturday night the Irishman disappeared with his share of gold to Sutter's Mill. He got drunk and revealed all our business, plans, rules and so forth. The next Monday we marked out new claims [f 182] and started digging. It was hard work, because the gold was deep in the rocks, but on the other hand there was a lot of it. It was in big nuggets, though it took most of the week to get to it. Every day more and more armed men came by to make inquiries, as before, but they were so familiar with our affairs that by Saturday the gunmen had set up camp beside us. I thought I knew what they had in mind and warned our party to be very circumspect, and not to give them any excuse to bother us.

We were all getting our ore together, and it was very rich. We were hoping for even better results than the week before. At about 10 a.m., a hundred of those soulless bandits invaded our claims, while we were down in them. They were so courteous as to ask who was the leader of our party. I was pointed out to them [f 183]. Their leader and eight others came over to where I was working — there were already four of them standing around me — all with pistols in their belts and Bowie knives. A few had rifles, others picks and shovels.

The leader and two men with picks got down into the hole to talk to me. He gave me to understand that the claim was his, because they had staked out from one side of the river to the other a couple of months before we came. He said a few more things in English which I didn't understand, but the gist of it was, the claim was his.

I was excited and answered him harshly. Fortunately he didn't understand me, and with a moment to reflect, I realized the gold wasn't worth risking my life. The rest of the invaders took over the other claims in the same manner. My companions ran back to our camp [f 184] for weapons before I got there, and I could see they were going to fight. They had already called for the horses to be brought in to saddle when I arrived and begged them to be calm. I pointed out that any resistance would be futile. As far as I was concerned, I was through with panning for gold. We saddled up and abandoned the place. The whole party dispersed. I rode back to Los Angeles with as little delay as possible.

Before I leave this disquisition on placer mining in California, I want to add a curious incident. One of my servants, Benito Pérez, whom I have mentioned before, brought his wife with him. When we arrived at Stanislaus, we arranged to pay her half an ounce of gold a day to cook and wash for us. Of my four servants, only the two *Mudos* Indians remained as such. [f 185] The other two panned gold on their own account, owing me for travel expenses to the placers.

Pérez's wife cooked a little extra at every meal and sold the leftovers to whomever asked. The business paid well, and before long she was buying on her own account meat, beans and other foodstuffs. She established a price of one peso for a small plate of frijoles and a flour tortilla, the same for fresh or dried meat and a tortilla. Business became so good she was taking in three or four ounces a day. She weighed the gold on a scale made of a Nantes sardine tin, a stick, and a flattened bullet, which it may be assumed, was not a very accurate scale and tended to favor Pérez's wife.

Afterwards [f 186] she lowered her prices to meet the competition. Even so, when we all gave up and went back to Los Angeles, she weighed her gold on my good set of scales, and it turned out she'd made a profit of thirteen pounds, seven ounces of gold with two or three months' work. This, in addition to what I have said already, should give an idea of the abundance of gold and how cheap it was.

[XIV]

Everyone knows the lawyer Cosmé Peña came to California with us in the colony. Some time afterwards he was named legal assistant by the central government to replace Rafael Gómez, who was suspended by Governor Victoria. After that he took a very active part in the Monterey rebellion against Nicolas Gutíerrez, which temporarily gained him the post of government secretary. In the counterrevolution of Monterey against Alvarado, he was one of the ringleaders, if not the main power behind it. However, he managed to get on the right side [f 187] of the government again, and Alvarado appointed him prefect of Los Angeles from 1838-1839—an appointment which was never confirmed by the central government.

Cosmé Peña was an ignorant man; no better than a shyster. His character was unreliable, his habits dissipated, particularly in the matter of drunkenness. The following verses of the famous ballad written by Don Luis Castillo Negrete about the Triumvirate of 1846 refer to him:

> A philosopher is he,
> Next in the triumvirate,
> Of California state.
> Sunk in iniquity,
> He wants to dominate;
> Though he's nothing but a louse
> In lots of mescal soused,
> He fancies himself wise.
> Yet in vain the fool tries
> To govern his own house.

The last line refers to the shame [crossed out and "state" substituted] of his family. I believe that to be the reason his wife left him to go back to Mexico with a servant, [f 188] undertaking the rigors of the journey by land at the risk of their lives. When they reached San Diego they joined two other people and made for the Colorado River, crossing the Cuyamaca Sierra. Cupeño Indians ambushed them in the desert, killed the three men and took Señora Peña captive.

In February of 1839, I led an expedition to Sonora, consisting of Luis Arenas, Matías Sabiche (an Italian sailor), two French sailors and four servants. We went with a guide.

Formerly, the Amajanes, Cochanes [sic] and Yuma Indians came to Los Angeles from time to time to trade hides and *tirutas*, black-and-white, hand-woven blankets of fine quality.[1] The Indians made them from the wool of wild sheep they hunted in the Sonoran territory, and the *tirutas* were much valued by ranchers for saddleblankets. [f 189] The Indians wanted horses and mares in exchange for the blankets, so they came every year at certain seasons, led by their chiefs. The local authorities gave them a horse or other beast and used clothing as a present. It was in this way that Luis Arenas and I became acquainted with the principal chiefs of that area. Since they knew we were going to Sonora, they prepared a reception for us at Pozo de los Indios. We encountered some three hundred Indians dressed in their most formal attire: body paint and feather headdresses, armed with bow and arrows.

From San Felipe on, Chief One-Eye Joe, who spoke Spanish, came with us and interpreted. Of the major chiefs, there was also Charagüe of the Yumas; Guatabalote ("Bareback Horse"), chief of all the Amajanes tribes, [f 190] who also had only one eye; Chief Coyote of the Cajuenes; Martin Cartridge and Black Stones, chiefs of villages at the mouth of the river; and others, among them Chief Francisco of Baja California.

As soon as we arrived the crowd of Indians yelled like demons in our honor, which was terrifying, considering we were at the mercy of these savages. But they proved to be friendly, and after a conversation through the interpreter we pitched camp about two hundred yards from theirs. We gave them twenty mares to butcher, which they ate up in no time.

During the night Chief Joe told me there was a white woman with them, another chief's captive. I tried to find out who she was, but I couldn't. I asked Chief Joe privately to point her out to me the next day. My curiosity grew as we made our preparations to set out. I joined [f 191] Chief Joe, and we went to the Indian encampment. He pointed out the white woman in a circle of Indians eating meat, but I couldn't tell her from the others, because she was dressed just the same, her hair cut straight across the forehead and black stripes painted on her face. She was wrapped in a rabbit skin cloak, with rags of something like petticoats underneath.

I hung around with various excuses, to see if I could get a word with her. I noticed she was watching me fixedly. She nodded her head as if in greeting, but Captain Joe had warned me not to speak to her. I went back to our camp, finding everyone ready to leave. I told Joe that if he stayed and was able to find out only the woman's name and where she was from, I'd give him a horse. At the moment, everyone was leaving. The Indians were for the most part gathered around us to say goodby. The party to which the woman belonged was the first to leave. It was clear she was being watched, and it would have been dangerous to gain the ill will of the tribe, [f 192] but from what Captain Joe said as we marched along, I presumed, though I was not sure, she was Cosmé Peña's wife.

My guess was confirmed afterwards, around 1840 or the beginning of 1841. A Sonoran arrived with some Indian children he'd acquired on the way, among them a girl of twelve or fourteen. I acquired her as a houseservant[2], had her baptized Encarnación, and in subsequent conversations with her I learned her father, the chief, had a white wife. From what she was able to tell me of the woman, it was positive that it was Peña's wife. I informed Don Juan Bandini and Don Matías Moreno, who lived near the border, of what I had heard, so they could investigate. But I never found out any more about the matter.

While I was on my way to Sonora, Ensign Macedonio González was persecuting the Indian villages he considered [f 193] guilty of murdering a family on one of Don Pío Pico's ranches. First he killed the men, then he took the women captive, while burning and sacking everything. When the pursuit was hot after them, they believed it was because of the women, so they killed them too. Three of the chiefs implicated in the matter, Martin Cartridge, Black Stones and Francisco, joined Bareback Horse and Coyote to go to Sonora, saying they wanted to visit the great chief, who was at that time Manuel Gandara.

Luis Arenas and I couldn't escape their company, so they went with us. During the journey I discovered that they had played a principal part in the above-mentioned crimes. It occurred to me that when we got to Sonora I could have them arrested and punished, but I didn't, because I had to return through the lands of their tribes.

On our way back I realized how right I had been [f 194] not to betray them. A short time after I left Sonora, the Papago Revolt took place. At Tule Lake, two days' ride from the Colorado River, the six of us were camped with seven Indian chiefs and their wives. A Cajuen appeared with a message for his chief that the Cucapas and Maricopas had attacked the Yuma village on the ford where we had to cross the river. (3) They had killed many people, and Chief Charagüe had to abandon the ford to his enemies. They had been waiting for us in order to kill us and the other chiefs, but now had returned to their villages until the full moon; precisely the night we were to ford the river.

Anyone who wanted to cross the Colorado tried to do it at the full moon in order to see if there were enemies in ambush. The tribes were generally at war with each other [f 195] and planned attacks for the full moon.

In view of this information, the Indians consulted with each other about what ought to be done — not for themselves, because they knew ways around — but because Chief Bareback Horse in particular didn't want to abandon us.

They asked Arenas and me if we could hurry up the march so as to ford the river one day before the full moon. Arenas wanted to go back, but Felipe Castillo and I and our servants resolved to go forward. The rest finally agreed to come too. We cleaned our guns -- which amounted to one flintlock, one rifle, one double-barrelled shotgun and two pair of pistols. We made up cartridges and set out, marching all night and all the next day to arrive at the river at about four in the afternoon. We spent the night making a raft of tule reeds and crossed the river at dawn, with saddles and equipment and all. The men [f 196] swam holding onto the raft. Guided by two Indians we put ourselves at the mercy of the current, which carried us three miles. The Indians took charge of getting the few horses across to endure the forced march. We had also left a great deal of baggage along the way.

On the other side, Cartucho and I and the two guides had to go on foot to pick up the horses, about a mile and a half upstream from us. Two of the best were missing, which put us in a critical and dangerous position. Chief Bareback Horse, or Guatabalote, tracked them and found one of the Indians who had stolen them. The chief clubbed him to death in front of us before we could intervene.

All together again, the Indians helped us harness and saddle quickly. Then they took their [f 197] way home upriver, and we went on to Los Angeles.

The next morning at the Alamo, we saw hostile Indians coming to cut off our retreat. We hastened our march and lost them to view by midday.

A busy corral at Los Angeles, see p.71

[XV]

For four or five years after the discovery of gold, Los Angeles was overrun with gamblers, fugitives and criminals of all countries. In self-defense, law-abiding citizens formed a volunteer police force that was very effective. In those times several outlaws from the north ended up here. One of the most notable was Murrieta and his band. We knew that some of them, possibly the leader himself, visited the city and committed crimes.

General Bean, whom the Californians called General Frijoles, was assassinated at this time at Mission San Gabriel. It was discovered that the cause of his death was [f 198] an Indian woman he had taken out of the canebrakes by force, because she had resisted.[1]

Bean's friends, Doctor Hope and Doctor Overstreet in particular, took great pains to find out exactly who committed the murder. They and other friends armed themselves to apprehend the suspects, and the matter became so serious Anglos and Californios alike were alarmed.

It was agreed, therefore, to name a committee to investigate and make the results public. The committee was made up of Americans and Californians: Alexander Bell, Doctor Overstreet, another American, Manuel Requeña and I. I didn't want to serve, because I have always been against any measures that depart from legal precedent, but I was given to understand the committee was purely one of inquiry. Testimony would be taken and made public, so as to avoid [f 199] any imputation of partiality on one side or the other. Finally I agreed to serve. At this point, the pursuit of Murrieta and his band had already begun.

The night of the murder of General Bean, Pancho Daniel the outlaw was asleep in a hut at Mission San Gabriel. Also at the Mission was Antonia la Molinera, a woman Murrieta was reputed to take with him dressed as a man.

Bean's murder took place right next to the place where Antonia was. Doctor Hope had made several arrests on suspicion, among them one Sandoval, a Sonoran. When they took him away, he said to Antonia, "San Cayetano is a good saint." [Translator's note: this is a word play on "callate," Spanish for "shut up."]. We proceeded to interrogate all the prisoners arrested on Antonia's word, such as Reyes, another whose name I forget, and Sandoval.[2] Dr. Hope had them in custody, and before we took their declarations he had threatened them and even [f 200] applied torture. Apparently Reyes and the other ones were implicated in the deaths or murders of Americans, but not in Bean's. Dr. Hope was determined on revenge at all costs. He insisted that if we couldn't clarify exactly which of them was the assassin, Sandoval should be hanged.

When the committee had finished its investigation, the results were turned over to the vigilantes.[3] Although we didn't think they justified the death penalty even for Sandoval, the people resolved to hang all three of them for the murders they had confessed. At this tense moment a man named Veruman committed a murder in Los Angeles while drunk, and was arrested in the act. They added him to the hanging with no further formalities, and all four were executed on the hill of the fort, the — of — of 185-. * [in English, in bottom margin] * *will try to find the date.* [4]

The identities of Murrieta's band were learned from la Molinera's testimony [f 201]. One of them was Flores. The first of the band to fall victim to popular justice, he was executed in Los Angeles even before the above-mentioned hanging. [5] The rest were pursued. La Molinera was not a prisoner, but was kept in a house under guard in case one of the band might kill her.

Pancho Daniel was caught, the second of Murrieta's men, the — of — of 185 -. [6] Popular feeling did not run quite as high since Murrieta himself and some of his men had been killed, so Daniel was given a legal trial and allowed a defense lawyer named Columbus Sims. Apparently there was some difficulty getting a guilty verdict, in spite of Daniel's notorious crimes.* [marginalia in English: *the lawyer obtained a change of venue. I will try to find this date/Savage] The people, morally certain of [f 202] his guilt, the morning of — of — of 185 - formed a lynching party including the principal merchants. They armed themselves, stormed the jail, took Daniel out and hanged him from the gateway of a corral next to the jail. [7]

The whole gang, according to Antonia la Molinera, was dead -- some had been executed by popular justice, some by Murrieta himself -- all except for one who emigrated to Sonora.

According to her story, the breakup was due to her. Pancho Daniel, the second in command, had seduced her away from Murrieta, and left the band with her. It appears that Murrieta swore vengeance on Daniel and la Molinera. She turned him in in self-defense, knowing that Murrieta, her former lover, had first sent [f 203] a man named Vergara to kill her. Vergara deserted, however, and got a job on the ranch of Palos Verdes (Wilmington). Murrieta sent another man after him, but this one turned up murdered a few days later, across from the present Convent of the Sisters of Charity, on what is now Alameda Street, near the main sewer.

A while after this, an Englishman or Scotsman named Dr. Wilson and another man arrived at the ranch and asked for a servant to accompany them. Vergara volunteered, and the three of them set off. One had a double-barreled shotgun which he gave Vergara to carry. The two men went ahead; Vergara was behind them. About six or seven miles from the ranch, Vergara shot the other man from behind, killing him instantly. Dr. Wilson ran all the way to Los Angeles and pressed charges. [f 204] When the body was recovered, it had been robbed of money and valuables.

Vergara remained at large, although he was pursued with a vengeance. He fled to Sonora and ended his life violently. I don't remember if he was murdered or shot by the garrison of the fort. [8]

[XVI]

A Californian from the north named * ——— was convicted of horse theft. He swore that whenever he got out of San Quentin he'd wreak vengeance on the person responsible for his capture. This was the year of 185 -. When his sentence ran out, he headed straight for Los Angeles to carry out his promise, lying in wait for Mr. ———.[1] At the same time he joined another criminal and seduced four or five young Angelenos called———[bottom margin, in English] * Presume it was Anastasio García. I understood that the party consisted of thirteen men, among them Pancho Daniel, Juan Flores, Espinosa, Andrés Fontes, Chigo Varelas, One-eye Pugunini (who later escaped to Sonora), Faustino García . . . [at least one line cut off.][2]

[f 205] They formed a gang and began to commit some small robberies -- stealing horses and so forth. Their intended victim left Los Angeles for San Juan with a cart, transporting some goods for hire. The gang followed him, but as luck would have it, missed him on the road. They heard he was at San Juan Capistrano and rode there, catching sight of him by afternoon. The intended victim became suspicious and informed Don Juan Foster, who I believe helped him escape that night over the Sierra del Trabuco to Temascal.

The gang, which had baptized itself "The Handcuffs" with their own password, went looking for him at the store where his cart was standing and didn't find him. After a few words between them and the Jew who kept the store, they killed the Jew and robbed the store. They spent most of the night there shouting and threatening the terrorized residents.

[f 206] When this news reached Los Angeles, Sheriff James Barton got up a posse of seven or eight well-armed men to pursue them.* [Bottom margin, in English] * Among Barton's party were: Frank Alexander, Hardy, Constable William H. Little, Constable Charles R. Baker, a Frenchman named François, and a blacksmith.[3]

People told Barton he didn't have enough men, but he said he thought there were enough. The outlaws' intended victim went with them. On the way to San Juan Capistrano there is a place called Barranco de los Alisos, between the ranches of San Joaquin and San Miguel, where the gang was hidden.[4] Probably they saw the posse coming; probably the posse had no idea they were there, riding unsuspectingly along in ones and twos. When Barton's men reached the edge of the barranco, the outlaws ambushed them with gunfire. Barton was killed, as was William H. Little and Charles D. Baker.[5] [f 207] The rest escaped the way they came, among them the intended victim of the outlaws. If he hadn't had a good, fast horse, they would have caught him, because they chased the posse for several miles.

This outrage greatly alarmed almost everyone. Since the outlaws were Californians, the Americans and foreigners supposed the Californian population must support them, which produced a dangerous division between the groups. None of it was true, however, because the influential Californians, especially Don Tomás Sánchez and

Don Andrés Pico, set out with a posse of Californians and didn't stop until they caught the outlaws in the sierra of Santiago. They found themselves obliged to execute a couple of them in San Juan Capistrano; the rest were sent to Los Angeles where the people judged them and hanged them on the hill where the jail is now.[6]

I think two or three of the gang members escaped this time, but due to the [f 208] zeal and energy of the new sheriff, Tomás Sánchez, they were caught and hanged at last.[7]

This put an end to the unrest and effected a reconciliation between the Americans and Californios. Any and all criminals were promptly captured during this period. It is well known that Sr. Sánchez, who was quite rich and popular among the Californians, * [bottom margin] (* the grandson of Don Vicente Sánchez, a major figure in Los Angeles) had always at his orders a considerable number of men paid by him.[8]

To tell the truth, there was also an American lawyer in Los Angeles, Joseph Lancaster Brent, known for his ability, honesty and popularity with all ranks of society, even the Americans. He was a young man, but one of the most prominent to exercise his profession here. In these critical times he was a leader [f 209] of the country, and his advice and help obviated many of the difficulties which might have had dreadful consequences. The name of Brent is engraved on the hearts of the most distingushed Californians, as a tribute to his merit and his services.[9]

One or two of the Murrieta band were caught in San Gabriel by a civilian posse headed by Captain Dorsey and Doctor Osborn. It was said these two cut off the head of one outlaw and displayed it as an object of scorn.[10] Without mentioning the judgment of Providence, I will say that afterwards the captain was murdered by his father-in-law[11] and the doctor had an attack of paralysis. The latter was obliged to be wheeled in a chair through the streets, avoided by decent people.[12]

Doctor Hope died miserably of drink at Mission San Fernando.[13]

If I remember correctly, Doctor Overstreet and his companion (Beard?), who greatly contributed [f 210] to the lynching of Sandoval, were killed by a lawyer named Watson at a dance given by various prominent people at the house of Don Abel Stearns. Overstreet and about twenty-odd others tried to crash the party, firing several shots through the window which wounded the lawyer Norton in the arm, and endangered the ladies. As luck had it, the only man at the party with a gun was Watson, or there would have been more bloodshed.[14] After this incident the good offices of Brent were instrumental in calming passions and preventing the matter from going further.

Party crashers
at Los Angeles

[f 211]

[XVII]
THE MISSIONS

In 1834 there were twenty-one missions in California. Some had still not been secularized. Although the padres who administered them knew they had no future, by and large they followed the system set up by the founders. This meant that the interested traveler could compare the padres' missions with those run by government-appointed administrators.

It is a well-known fact that the California missions and the other missions in frontier territory were founded by the Franciscan Fathers and other conventual orders of that time.

California fell to the lot of the Regular Franciscans. They were to propagate the faith among the heathen, with no half measures, at the risk of their lives. With the help of the king of Spain, they founded a system of missions worthy of admiration, which for many years was the only resource of the country.

[f 212] The system was as follows:

The population of neophytes was divided between married and singles.

Married couples lived in villages and received a weekly ration for their sustenance.

Bachelors slept in a separate building under the direct supervision of the Indian mayors, who locked them in each night and gave the key to the padre.

Unmarried girls slept in a different building, which was called the convent, in the charge of a matron; she also gave the key to the padre when the girls retired to sleep.

The Indians were divided into work crews: field hands, cowboys, craftsmen, hunters. Each crew had a boss, who reported to the padre.

The buildings of the missions were spacious blocks with apartments inside and one or two great doorways for general communication. Within the square was the house [f 213] of the padre, the first building you saw as you entered; the church was attached to it.

Off the inner courtyards were carpenter's and saddler's shops; weaving sheds for serge, blankets and rough cloth; the hatter's, tanner's, soapmaker's shops; the warehouse full of goods produced by the mission or bought from the trading ships; and also brick kilns and tile factories. Outside the quadrangle were pits for making adobe.

The public buildings were all adobe with wood and tile roofs, solidly built.

At the peremptory peal of bells in the morning, all the Indians got up and went to the church for a short prayer. Another bell, and the single people went to the refectory while the married ones went to their own houses for breakfast, all before sunrise.

[f 214] At the third bell the work crews reported to their assigned tasks.

I remember at Mission San Jose, at that period (1834-1835) the richest of them, Padre José María de Jesús González was the administrator; a capable man and absolutely honest. He dedicated himself to maintaining the system adopted by his predecessors.

The farm laborers formed up in the corral with oxgoad and yoke; the straw boss in charge of the oxen told each of them which pair to yoke up and drive off. When all were ready, they were sent in groups wherever they were to work.

The workshops were under the supervision of a white director or of an Indian who had [f 215] mastered the craft. While the products were not perfect, the manufactures met the needs of the mission.

Agriculture also was well advanced, in spite of the lack of implements we have today. The main crops produced abundant harvests to feed the population of the mission with enough left to sell to the troops and the white settlers.

It is strange how those priests, with no more support than four or five so-called Californian soldiers, kept so many Indians in good order and commanded their respect at all times. It is true the Indians worked for the food, blankets and shirts issued to them (the women got cloth to make petticoats and shawls); their only education was moral doctrine — but [f 216] they still had great respect for all white people! They were organized into families, and that was progress in itself.

Other missions still under the control of padres were losing a sense of discipline, because the Indians were attracted by the idea of liberty inherent in secularization

The missions under lay administrators were even more difficult to run, with reason; but in my opinion, the majority of lay administrators took little care for the land nor for the indigenous people. They took advantage of their positions and of the government which depended on them for support — since they were all government appointees.

As the end result of the secularization (which may have been well-intentioned), the valuable land and twenty thousand Indian workers disappeared in a very short time.[1]

[f 217] My knowledge of the mission system of agriculture, industry and education was based on a book called *Country Living and Pastoralism*, containing all the information necessary to run the farms and govern the laborers. This idea was based on some conversations I had with Padre José María Zalvidea at Mission San Juan Capistrano.[2]

This padre was responsible for the flourishing state of Mission San Gabriel at its peak. A man of talent and education, he at the same time was very liberal in his views.

When Don Agustín Janssens took over the mission in 184_?, I spent nearly a year there and had the opportunity to speak often with Padre Zalvidea.[3] By then he was very old and completely given over to religious devotion; apart from the hours strictly necessary to eat and sleep, he spent all his time praying and reading devotional books. This he did walking up and down the interior patio of the mission. Almost daily he suffered periods of mental confusion, when [f 218] he stamped on the ground, scratching his head with one hand and holding the book in the other, crying out, "Ah, Satan, I've caught you and I'm going to give you such a whipping!" and similar exclamations. Afterwards, he would go on with his prayers. At night with his evening prayers it was the same thing: when the fit came on him he would snatch up a whip of knotted cords, flailing the walls and furniture and shouting that he saw Satan. He also flagellated himself and wore several knotted horsehair cords around his body.[4]

When he came to the table this is how he dined: he had an antique pottery cup, horn utensils and a napkin he kept in his sleeve. He served himself some of everything on the table and mixed it all together in his cup: dessert, salad, wine and all. That was how he ate it. His conversation during the meal was pleasant, polite and instructive. At the end of the meal he wiped his own utensils; the plate and cup [f 219] were washed by the servants in his presence and taken immediately to his room.

Some of the Californians were of the opinion that he lost his mind because Mission San Gabriel was taken away from him when he tried to build an iron fence around all the cropland. When I saw the mission in 1838, the past splendor was still evident in the main vineyard, the separate garden plots of the soldiers, the orchard so there was always fruit for the guests, the padre's private garden where a few orange trees still stood. All around were planted olives and pomegranates, making a very beautiful picture. There were two grist mills; at one of them the inhabitants of Los Angeles ground their flour.[5] There was a small woods and garden plots on the grounds of this mill; the millpond that supplied the power and irrigation water still exists, the property of the Honorable B.D. Wilson.

All the missions had ranches, some farther and some nearer to the main quadrangle. They owned all the land along the coast, except for what belonged to the presidios, the three towns, and a royal concession ranch or two. Later, under colonial law, the ranches were distributed to private citizens. But while they were run by the missions, each ranch had a foreman, white or Indian. Some of them were large horse and cattle ranches; others raised sheep, others field crops only. Some ranches had both crops and livestock, in which case there was a foreman for each department. The Indian laborers lived in villages on the ranches, very much as in the mission itself.

[f 221] The morning's work went from sunrise to eleven-thirty or twelve. Then the workers came for the second meal of the day and went back to work at one or one-thirty until sunset if the days were short; if the days were long, they generally stopped an hour or so before sunset.

The workers were divided into groups, each with a straw boss. After each day's work was done, the straw boss reported to the foreman, who reported to the padre, and received the task for the following day.

The last of the three daily meals came at the end of the day, consisting of corn or wheat and beans cooked together, called *pozole*; sometimes in the morning they got *atole* and meat. *Atole* was corn cooked with lime, washed well, and ground into a paste. [f 222] The paste was dissolved and boiled. The women did the grinding.

The married couples received a weekly ration of corn, wheat and beans, with a daily dole of meat, usually jerkey.

The women also harvested and hulled seeds, pruned grapevines, carded and spun wool, and sometimes hauled clay for the tile factory, especially the unmarried girls, who were always kept busy.

On Sunday, the day of rest, the Indians assembled in clean shirts, blankets and loincloths to attend high mass. The Indians themselves provided the instrumental and vocal music, some of them very good singers. There was an Indian called Antero at Mission Santa Barbara, who lived until about 1843; he had an extraordinary tenor voice that filled the whole church and astonished the Europeans. He also played the [f 223] violin.[6]

Mass included a sermon, part of it in the language of the Indians of the mission, as Padre Zalvidea preached it. If the padre didn't speak the Indian language, he would have an interpreter explain the doctrine. But most of the Indians knew enough Spanish to understand what was said to them.

The tribunal that punished the Indians' sins was the padre in charge. He listened to any complaints from the mayors, foremen or others in authority. He passed sentence of the stocks, or whipping, or handcuffs or leg irons. There was always a jail with such implements at hand, for the securing of delinquents.

When a whipping was indicated, the victim was tied to a post, or stretched face-down on the ground. His loincloth was removed and his shirt pulled up. Then the mayor or foreman applied the number of lashes the padre ordered, with rod or lariat, to the buttocks or lower back. Generally [f 224] punishment took place in the guardroom, next to the jail cell, in sight of the main buildings.

Each mission had an infirmary, a long gallery with pallets for the sick Indians. Sometimes the padres themselves prescribed medicines, but the Indians preferred their own "medicine men," old men who knew from tradition or had learned by themselves how to treat certain illnesses.[7]

When I first visited the missions I never saw a school. Afterwards a few of them had schools. Nevertheless, every mission had a few Indians who could read and write somewhat, and understood music, because the padres themselves or someone attached to the mission taught them.

It should be noted that this system declined so rapidly that in 1840 it had almost disappeared, and most of the Indians with it. It is also true that in 1834 the pox invaded [f 225] northern California, especially Sonoma, decimating the Indian population; but the epidemic did not reach the south. What destroyed many Indians was abandoning them to their own devices with no protection from themselves. The result was drunkenness and corruption. Venereal disease, which had always been a problem, developed with a vengeance and caused great suffering and death. Here in Los Angeles the Indians died like animals with no one to care for them, and it was the same in the other towns and ex-missions converted to villages.

Perhaps this was due to the primary education given the Indians, which never was meant to prepare them to live on their own or look after themselves. They were treated as perpetual children, subject to guardians.

The padres' corporal punishment was also applied by the lay administrators of the missions, the mayors and councilmen, and [f 226] even the masters the Indians worked for. Each had arrogated the right to punish and whip the Indians under him.

[XVIII]
DAILY LIFE

When the Híjar-Padrés colony arrived in California, the total population loosely called "white" [*gente de razón*] was no more than five thousand including the garrisons.

The education of the inhabitants consisted generally of Catholic doctrine introduced by the padres. The same padres taught one or two Californians to write, after a fashion.

In the presidios there were a few Californians with a little more primary education: reading, writing and the rudiments of arithmetic, as well as the doctrine which formed the principal, or essential, branch of instruction. Even this small advance was due to the military officers resident in the presidios, who had been educated elsewhere; or learned from contact with [f 227] the old Spanish officers and the merchants and others who came on ships. To this nucleus add the arrival of Mexican families, well educated and soon scattered throughout the country.

In the interior settlements there were very few people who could be said to write and figure. Even after the arrival of intelligent and educated people, education remained at a low level.

The women learned even less, because they had been convinced that book-learning was bad for girls; they could barely read, let alone write. But in spite of their lack of education, the ladies were highly moral, diligent and clean, dedicated to their household duties; some even carried out duties that properly belonged to men. These women were charitable and hospitable; they didn't care to sell food [f 228] but shared among families, one supplying what another might lack.

A traveler could go up to any house in California, confident he could stay however many days he liked and pay nothing for roof, bed, food and even horses to continue his journey. But the mothers took great care of their daughters, and the traveler often met only the men of the family.

The men busied themselves almost exclusively with livestock, which meant they only worked at certain times, such as the roundup and branding, or slaughtering time. The hides and tallow were their income as well as all the coinage there was at that time.

The Californians were not much given to farming, because they could buy grain at the missions. [f 229] A few grew crops for their families only — but as the missions declined, agriculture of necessity became more widespread.

The men who were already full grown in that epoch kept the character of their Spanish ancestors. They were upright and honorable men, imperious, and their word without documents or witnesses was good for any amount of money. This character also declined rapidly as what was termed "enlightenment" arose.

The most important family value was respect for the head of it — to the point where the parents still governed married sons and daughters, who had to submit humbly to punishment still.

Daughters had very little choice of husbands. The parents arranged marriages [f 230] for young people before they even met each other.

Young married couples lived with one or the other set of parents, just as if they were still minors. They helped with the work, and the parents provided for all.

Just what relations were is impossible to calculate. The inhabitants of California were all related to each other, by law and by custom.

Religious education was observed in all homes. Before dawn each morning a hymn of praise was sung in chorus; at noon, prayers; at about six p.m. and before going to bed, a rosary and another hymn. I saw on several occasions at balls or dances when the clock struck eight, the father of the family stopped the music and said the rosary with [f 231] all the guests, after which the party continued. I saw the same thing sometimes at roundups, when the old men stopped work to pray at the accustomed hours, joined by all present.

When young people met their godparents anywhere, they were obliged to take off their hats and ask a blessing. The godparents' obligation was to substitute for the parents if they should die, if necessary provide for the godchild's keep and education, and give good advice.

The *compadrazgo* was a relationship between the parents and godparents of the child, ties recognized by the Church but not by civil law. At every baptism the priest explained the obligations [f 232] entailed by the relationship.

When two men were united in a friendship superior to the common run, they called each other *valedor*—this term was often used among the ranchers as a term of appreciation and trust.

Women's work was harder, longer and more important than men's. They were in charge of the kitchen. They made all their clothes, which was a laborious task because the petticoats were edged with lace or embroidered with cutwork in the most exquisite fashion. They were also fond of fine bed linens, and the sheets and pillowcases had to be lace-edged or embroidered too. Since clothing was expensive, they turned and altered used clothing until it was almost new. Most of them ironed the clothes with their hands, patting and stretching the fabric until it was perfectly smooth. They also sewed exquisite clothes for their husbands, fathers and brothers: broadcloth jackets with worked buttonholes, embroidery on some of them, braid and trapunto on others. Vests were generally [f 233] made of silk or wool, embroidered in colors; the short breeches also. The sleeves on riding jackets, made of wool or corduroy, were trimmed with velvet, corduroy or fringe.

The women also had to comb the menfolks' hair every day and tie it up.

Many women also baked bread, made candles and ordinary soap, and some I knew brought in the harvest and threshed the grain.

With regard to the clothing I described above, I was referring to families who enjoyed a good economic position. Poor people wore [f 234] the same kind of clothes, but made of cheaper material. Poor women probably worked even harder than rich women.

The clothes worn by well-off ladies of 1834 and 1835 were a short narrow tunic of silk or organdy, a high tight bodice trimmed with silk ribbons or flowers according to the caprice of the lady, and red flannel (or another color) underneath according to taste. A shawl, similar to the Spanish mantilla, was also worn, and low cloth slippers.

The hair was pulled back smoothly and braided, tied with ribbon and a small ornament or silk flower, very prettily.

The final touch was a silk handkerchief at the neck, the ends crossed and tied in front. Some women used a camorra, which was a black silk handkerchief tied gracefully around the head.

[f 235] We have already mentioned that men's work was exclusively on the ranches. Some grew crops, but there was no market except what they might sell to the presidios.

Men's clothing consisted of knee breeches, slit six inches on the outer side and adorned with ribbon or braid, and four to six silver buttons (or other metal, depending on the individual's relative prosperity); the fly front had another such button, almost the size of a peso.

A long vest of wool, silk, velvet, or corduroy (according to economic circumstances), variously adorned, was worn under a longer jacket of the same material and adorned in the same style.

High-heeled boots were made of a whole tanned deerskin, dyed black or red and tooled or embroidered with silk according to the preference of the individual. The leather had a lace or [f 236] drawstring to put the foot into; then it was rolled down to a little below the knee, covering the calf and half the instep, and tied with the lace.

To go with the boot, shoes were made of what was called *berruchi*, four to six pieces of red and black calfskin or suede with an embroidered vamp. The sole was a single thickness of flexible calfskin to grip the stirrup securely. The toe had a point, turned upward, to keep the *tapaderos* of the stirrups from rubbing the shoe.

The hat was broad-brimmed with a round crown, stoutly made of wool. It was kept on with a chin strap two inches wide, formed into a big rosette under the chin. Almost all the men covered their heads with a black bandanna [f 237] tied like an Andalusian peasant.

The saddle had a big rough wooden tree, strong enough to stand hard use. Underneath it was padded with calfskin; cowhide thongs secured it to the horsehair cinch. A square of tooled calfskin went over the saddle and over that a larger hide, more finely carved, embroidered with silk or even silver or gold, and nearly covered the horse on both sides. These were called the *corazas*. There was also a matching crupper and saddlebags to carry necessities.

The most important item [f 238] for any Californian was the lariat. This was made of four or six one-half-inch-wide rawhide strips, plaited and worked until the lariat was perfectly flexible. When it was not needed, it was tied to the back of the saddle with a special strap; when in use, it hung on the pommel.

The knife was also of first importance. It was carried in a sheath on the outside of the right boot, fastened to the bootlace.

Every man had a sword, though the civilians hadn't much use for it, carried on the left of the saddle under the leg.

The serape was also indispensable, and much more useful. When not worn, it was rolled and tied behind the saddle with the lariat.

In the hazards of ranch work, if it happened a man had to spend the night out, the saddle served for a pillow, the *corazas* and saddlebags for a bed, the serape for a blanket.

[f 239] This same Californian, if he had to go on a campaign to fight Indians, or for military service, added a long padded leather coat of seven layers which covered him from neck to knee. This *cuera*, as it was called, provided protection from arrows. A small oval shield, concave on the inside, presenting the convex side to the enemy, could be slipped on the left arm.

The usual weapon was an old flintlock shotgun, perhaps a lance, or a pair of pistols. This last was very unusual, and only the leaders carried pistols, but every man had a good Spanish blade from Toledo.

Officers wore the same dress, distinguished only by their insignia of rank.

All these customs eventually changed, particularly after the arrival of the colonial families from Mexico. The Californians took up the long pants buttoned from hip to ankle on both sides, low boots, short jacket [f 240] and the low-crowned, wide-brimmed white felt hat and Mexican saddle.

The ladies exchanged their fitted dresses for voluminous ones, took out their braids and piled their hair up elaborately, held with small combs instead of the large one they had used up until then. Women of modest means, and usually the older women of any economic level, wore petticoats of suitable material (instead of the tunic) from the waist down. The blouse had sleeves below the elbow, and the neck and chest were covered with a black silk or cotton kerchief folded diagonally and tied in back; the front was pinned to the waist of the petticoat.

The small town women continued using the shawl, of linen or cotton, and homemade shoes called *berruchis* because they were pointed like the men's, only smaller, with a point at the heel too. All women usually wore stockings, leaving no part of themselves uncovered but face and hands — any more display was considered immodest.

[XIX]
AMUSEMENTS

[f 241] The principal amusement of the Californians was horse racing, on which they wagered (for their means) enormous sums. Some would bet the horse they were riding, saddle and all.

There was also the game of *gallo* played on horseback: a live rooster was buried in the sand up to its neck. The riders withdrew a hundred yards or more, then came at full speed, leaning from the saddle [f 242] to snatch up the rooster. The one who succeeded was the winner. This was a dangerous sport requiring great agility; the rooster would often duck his head so it was very difficult to grab it at full gallop.

There was also the bullfight. For this a large ring was fenced with tin sheets or heavy rails. Outside it a pavilion shaded with branches served for the families and other spectators. The bull was lassoed by the horns and dragged into the ring and released. There were a hundred or more mounted men in the ring; that many or more outside it. The more skilful ones, usually prominent ranchers, caped the bull with their serapes, and one would prick him with the lance. When the bull was tired and losing enthusiasm, the gate was opened and the bull herded out at a run with all the mounted men [f 243] after him. The object was to seize the bull's tail and upset him; but in order to do it, each of the mob of riders jostled and trampled each other at great risk of life and limb, a dreadful sight.

Then another bull was brought, and so on, until the time allotted was up.

There were always horses and men hurt in these sports.

Another game played on horseback was *el juego de la vara*: the players formed a circle with the horses' heads towards the center. One man with a bundle of switches rode around outside the circle, and hit one man from behind with a switch. The favored man [f 244] at once chased after the first man with reckless speed, and if he caught him he beat him with switches. The first rider evaded him with skillful horsemanship, until he could find a place in the circle. They kept this up for hours. The point was for the man being pursued not to allow the pursuer to touch him. If he was clumsy, he was well switched.

On major holidays they used to lasso bears and take them in carts to town to fight bulls. The bull's foreleg was tied to the bear's paw with a rope about ten yards long so they had to fight. Sometimes the bear won, sometimes the bull; I saw both cases. It was a pretty brutal spectacle, but people were used to it and didn't see anything wrong with such fights.

[f 245] There were also cockfights, as in Mexico and other places, with serious betting. Indians or foreigners might run foot races, but generally not Californians.

The Californians were fearless and expert horsemen, and to the spectator much of what they did was incredible. The ladies were for the most part excellent horse-women as well; I saw some of them lasso bulls, catch them by the tail and upset them, and even cape them — but not very many.

There were also dances, or *fandangos*, held on all possible occasions whether religious or profane. A great pavilion shaded with green branches was set up in front of the house where the dance was to take place. The inside of the pavilion was covered with white cloth adorned with ribbons, artificial flowers, etc. [f 246] It had three sides enclosed and the fourth open for the men on horseback to congregate; there were sawhorses placed firmly to keep the horses back. The ladies sat inside.

The music consisted of a violin and guitar, and two or three singers, at one end where they wouldn't be in the way. The master of ceremonies was called the *tecolero*, and he of course stood in the center to direct the dancing. He got the ladies to stand up when it was a "ladies only" dance, beginning at one end of the pavilion tapping his feet in time to the music, clapping his hands in front of a lady. She would get up, cross the ends of her shawl or kerchief, and take her place in the center. She picked up the edges of her petticoats and began a fancy dance to the music, making two or three circles [f 247] in the middle of the pavilion, and went back to her seat. The *tecolero* continued his office until all the ladies had had a turn — those who didn't want to dance, or didn't know how, stood up and made a graceful turn around the floor and sat down again.

If the piece was to be danced by couples, the men dismounted, and hung their spurs on the saddle horn, and entered the pavilion hat in hand. Each selected a partner and went to dancing for all he was worth. Meanwhile, the mounted men surged back and forth continually, shoving for a place at the rail. When the music stopped, the lady went back to her seat and the man got back on his horse.

The dances were called *sones*, more or less [f 248] in the same style but with variations in the tunes, words and ceremonies. I will explain some of the more common ones.

A fancy ball on the Old West Coast, after Wm. Meyers, 1846

[XX]
DANCES

LA JOTA — was the favorite popular dance of the country. Each man took a partner, placing her on his right, facing another couple. As many couples as fit into the available space could dance this, two lines facing each other. As soon as the music began, the singers started with the lyrics, and the dancers moved arms and hands as the spirit took them, as long as the verse lasted. Then the singers took up the chorus, and the dancers joined hands in two circles, one of men and one of women. The women's circle turned in the opposite direction from the men's, until each couple was again side by side and took their place in the line.

The singer sang the next [f 249] verse, then the chorus, and the figures of the dance followed as before. On the last verse, the dancers all performed the same movements.

The steps were as follows: pick up one foot and then the other in time to the music, hopping as in a folk dance. The *jota* was beautiful and graceful when performed perfectly, usually by older people — they knew it better, and the dance itself required a certain solemn dignity. The singers made up the lyrics as they went along, or maybe they were traditional. I will recite some common ones:

> *Verse for the First Figure:*
> Bend your knee to the ground
> Saying Jesus help me,
> To the Virgin of Zaragoza,
> And my guardian angel too.

[f 250] This verse was repeated twice for the first figure.

> *Refrain:*
> Know this, my life,
> How courteous I've been,
> How much I've respected you,
> How much I've loved.
> All of the gossips
> Who tried to find out
> And tell lies about us,
> Never could begin.
> Only the Court of Justice,
> Powerful and great,
> Put me in this prison,
> Where I must suffer,
> Where I must stay,
> A prisoner in irons,

By a woman betrayed.
Never you mind me,
Ungrateful one.
Some day in your dreams
You'll remember me,
I was your lover.

Another different verse followed in the same style, the dancers went through their figures, and the refrain came around again [f251] with different words.

LA BAMBA -- this dance was performed only by ladies who knew how, because the steps were complicated. The most expert could do it with a glass of water balanced on her head. The spectators might throw a knotted handkerchief on the ground as she danced —the lady picked it up with her feet without missing a beat and concealed it, with two or three more. Then, still to the music and without spilling a drop of water, she would deposit all the handkerchiefs on the ground again. At the conclusion of this performance, the *tecolero* took the glass of water off her head and she retired to her seat amid frenzied applause. Sometimes, in fact almost always when one of these famous dancers performed, the spectators threw money at her feet or put their hats [f252] on her head or in her hands. Some put their kerchiefs around her shoulders. Sometimes she was so loaded with pledges she had to stop dancing. The donors of hats, handkerchiefs, etc., redeemed them from the *tecolero* for money or a gift, large or small according to the means, position or intentions of the donor.

Lyrics of this dance:
La Bamba is tiny,
La Bamba's enormous,
The dearly beloved,
Consolation of sorrows.

It went on in this fashion, so it gives an idea of what the rhythm of the music was like.

LA ZORRITA—this is a dance for couples, like the *jota*, except that during the first verse the men pantomime the lyrics. For the refrain, two opposite couples [f253] join hands in a chain of four. On the second refrain, the men jump up and clap hands, acting out the different verses. The dancers sing too.

Words to this dance:
The little fox, ladies and gentlemen,
Went to the top of the hill,
To have a good time, a good time,
She came back with a skinful.

Refrain:
And saying she's falling, she feels
Just awful, because she is like
The sparks flying upward,
To the top of the tower they fly,
And the fox jumps up
And falls on the ground.
(This last part is where the men jump up and clap hands.)
The little fox, ladies and gentlemen,
Went to Perote,
To have a good time, a good time,
Came back with her hair in a bun.
(Here the man makes a gesture of putting his partner's hair up. The refrain is the same.)

[f 254] LOS CAMOTES -- this is similar to the previous dance, with verse and refrain, but different tune, words and steps.

Verse of this Dance:
The lovers got themselves lost,
Two police and a grenadier,
A corporal and an officer,
All went to look for them.

Refrain:
Tra-la-la, tra-la-la,
With hot pepper-ah,
Sugar and cloves,
With cinnamon sticks,
Tra-la-la, tra-la-la.
(repeat the above)

This is a very slow dance. At the end of the refrain the man salutes his partner and resumes his place to continue. The dancers sing as well.

EL BORREGO -- This was a dance for one couple, a man and a woman. It began with a *zapateado* [translator's note: the fast, foot-stamping type of tap dance associated with flamenco] to the music. As the singers come in, both dancers take out kerchiefs [f 255] and pantomime the song; for example, if the song says the ram lamb butts, the man makes a show of butting his partner; if the ewe lamb butts, the lady feigns a charge and the man capes her with the kerchief just as she did him.

Verse of this Song
Madam, your little lamb

wants to take me to the river
and I tell him no,
because it's much too cold.

Refrain:
Here comes the pretty one,
Here comes the ugly one,
And the little lamb
Comes out to play.
Here comes the black boy
With a big stick,
And the little lambkin
Butts whom he can:
Sometimes butts her,
Or sometimes him.
(This last part is where the kerchief is used.)

[f256] EL BURRO -- this was generally danced at the close of family reunions. An equal number of men and women form a circle, holding hands. In the center, one person, man or woman, is It, the burro. When the music starts, the people in the circle dance around the burro. Two or three verses were sung, and at a certain word each person embraced another of the opposite sex —whomever was left out, was It.
     The words were these if a man was It:

     I have a little basket
     Full of green chilis.
     Who told you to be the burro
     Of all the women?
Everyone was waiting for this verse to embrace each other:

     I have a little basket,
     All full of squashes,
     [f 257] Who told you to be the burro?
     Why don't you hug someone?
     Why don't you hug someone?
     (While the last line is repeated the dancers embrace.)

If a woman is It, the song goes like this:
     Try to examine
     Everyone's name,
     So as not to be the burro
     Among the men.

The refrain was always the same, and partners were changed throughout. Naturally there are many other versions of this dance and the others, but more or less similar to this example.

EL FANDANGO -- a man and a woman danced this. The man had to be good at it, because after beginning with castanets (or snapping his fingers) and dancing in place, he had several complicated steps around the floor while the music played and the verse and refrain were sung. [f 258] Then the music stopped, and the singer cried *"Bomba!"* At this, the man had to compliment his partner in extemporaneous verse as well as his wit served him. The music played again, another verse and refrain was sung, and then it was the woman's turn to direct a verse to the man. If she was too shy or didn't have any talent for poetry, he supplied a rhyme or two to fill the blank. Then the *tecolote* brought out another couple, or sometimes the same couple did another round.

The verses were something like this:

Oh, my hopeless love!
How shall I forget you?
If I tell you goodby,
I lose the glory of loving you.

REFRAIN:
Ay! Could it be a lie?
Ay! Could it be the truth?
These little dark-haired girls,
What a poor return they give!
Ay! Could it be a lie?
[f 259] Ay! Could it be the truth?

EL SARABE -- this is the national dance of the Mexican people. It has many variations, because different folk songs are combined in it; the music varies too, and it is very difficult to dance well. Each different movement requires different steps, so only experts used to try it.

The *tecolero* had to know who could do the *sarabe* well. He chose such a couple and invited them to the center of the floor and they danced. In the intervals between movements, to give them a rest, the singer improvised on the theme just played.

LA CONTRADANZA -- this was a dance belonging to the best society. Two lines were formed, one of men and one of women. The music was a slow waltz in 3/4 time. [f 260] The step was the dancers' choice and could be improvised, but was usually traditional. The young people didn't usually do this dance.

The old women also knew folk dances, like:

EL CABALLO -- a couple danced this. As soon as the music started they swayed back and forth and danced to one side and the other. According to the words, there was some business with kerchiefs, and at a given point, the woman caught up her skirt, front and back, and swished it, to give the idea of riding a horse. The man took his kerchief by two points to show he was holding the reins, and they stepped to the music like a horse trotting.

Verse of this Dance:
On horseback, with spurs,
I ride to see my sweetheart.
If anyone tries to stop me,
I have my lasso and a knife.

Refrain:
Oh, horse! Oh, rider!
The Devil's in it.
[f 261] Oh, horse! Oh, rider!

There were other dances of this sort, called *El Portorico, La Sarna, Los Juiles, Los Tejamaniles*, etc., etc.

[XXI]
BURIAL CUSTOMS

When someone died, a habit of Saint Francis was supplied for a shroud. If the habit was an old one worn by the Franciscan padres, all the better.[1] While the patient was still on his deathbed, they laid the habit on top of the blanket, certain he would gain more indulgences like that. There were always relatives and friends in the room or nearby, more and more of them, praying constantly.

After the person died, the habit was put on. The corpse was laid out on the floor with a stone at the head and four wax candles. From that moment on, the whole town with few exceptions was obligated to visit, attend the wake, and pray; this [f 262] went on almost without pause until the burial, accompanied by mournful hymns.

The corpse was laid on a table covered with black cloth. Four men, changing off from time to time, were pallbearers. The priest went before with the altar boys, stopping at intervals to sing responses for the soul of the deceased. When they got to the church, high or low mass (according to the family's means) was said over the corpse, with various prayers. At the end of this, the procession continued in the same fashion to the cemetery, with the empty coffin following. At the cemetery the body was put in the coffin, the priest said the final benediction, and the coffin was lowered into the grave. Since it was obligatory for the chief mourners to attend, as well as all the families of the town, including the women and children, there was plenty of weeping and wailing.

When the head of a family died, [f 263] people had to come for the funeral even from far away, so the body might be left unburied for two or three days.

Unmarried women, of whatever age, were dressed in white with a palm frond and a crown of flowers.

If it was a baby or toddler, there was a fiesta with dancing, dinner and drinks and rockets and gunfire, because it was believed that such a soul went straight to Heaven. The little corpse was dressed as an angel, or the saint he was named for, just as the parents or godparents decided; if it was a girl, she was dressed like an image of the Virgin or a female saint.

These customs to which I refer in my little memoirs disappeared gradually. The change began with the arrival of the colonists, most of whom came from Mexico City. The ladies adopted full skirts, [f 264] upswept hair styles and combs, silk kerchiefs and fine cloth shoes.

Some of the prominent men and ranchers adopted long pants instead of knee breeches, with high-heeled boots instead of gaiters; the saddle also underwent changes.

Proper schools were established; customs and amusements were considerably reformed.

When the Americans came into the country, we experienced the final changes noted to date.

Coronel's Mansion
　　　Los Angeles, Nov. 16 of 1877

Mr. H. H. Bancroft
San Francisco

My dear Sir. The arduous and gigantic project you have in your hands I hardly imagine
will profit you materially. But I am sure [f 265] your name will go down to posterity
as a genius among historians.
　　　This little memoir and product of a feeble recollection I hope will be useful to you
in some fashion. If such be the case I am entirely satisfied and recompensed.

　　　Your servant, respectfully,

　　　A.F. Coronel

NOTES

Chapter 1.

1 The *Morelos*, a 196-ton brig, was a corvette in the Mexican Navy, commanded by Lucas F. Manso. It departed San Blas on August 1, 1834, with José María Padrés and 100 colonists. It reached Monterey on September 24. Adele Ogden, "Trading Vessels on the California Coast, 1786-1848," p. 674, Ms., Bancroft Library.

2 On May 9, 1832, Brigadier General José Figueroa was appointed governor of Alta California, vested with both civil and military authority. He was "an able and prominent man," having served for five or six years in Mexico as commandant general of Sonora and Sinaloa. Unfortunately, shortly after taking up his post on January 14, 1833, Figueroa became ill. This led him to ask to be relieved on March 25. On July 15, José María Híjar was informed he would succeed to the governorship, but the appointment was later nullified. Already deeply involved in the colonization project for Alta California with José María Padrés, he welcomed the prospect of returning to California. However, when the Padrés-Híjar company reached Monterey in 1834, friction quickly broke out between Figueroa and the two leaders of the newly arrived colonists. So bitter did the dispute become that Figueroa finally arrested the two men and sent them back to Mexico to stand trial on charges of plotting revolution. Their bitter quarrel is detailed in Bancroft, *California*, III: 259-291.

3 Padrés became a lieutenant colonel in 1830 and came to California as assistant inspector of troops with the newly appointed governor, José María Echeandía. He subsequently served as inspector of customs and implemented the governor's decree of secularization of the missions. Under displeasure of the new governor, Manuel Victoria, Padrés was sent back to Mexico at the end of 1831. He then joined in establishing the colonization project which he headed with Híjar, a wealthy Mexican citizen. Bancroft renders this judgment: "Padrés was a man of remarkable energy, intelligence, and magnetism, a most radical republican in the Mexican sense of the term; and one whose influence was long felt in Cal[ifornia], through his teachings to the young men who later controlled the country. So well did they learn their lesson, indeed, in colony times they turned against their teacher when he seemed to have forgotten their claims to office." *Ibid.*, IV: 765.

4 This is not correct. There was no effort to recruit political dissidents. Instead, a general recruitment notice was issued for men, women, and families to join the colony. That some of the recruits might wish to leave Mexico for political reasons is probably true, but not under duress as suggested by Coronel. Hutchinson, *Frontier Settlement in Mexican California*, p. 196.

5 Juan Bandini was chosen to represent California in the Mexican Congress in 1833. He sailed on the brig *Catalina* for Acapulco on May 14 to take up his post. He took his oath of office in the Chamber of Deputies on July 23. He returned to California in 1834 with the Padrés-Híjar party on the *Natalia*. *Ibid.*, p. 187; Ogden, "Trading Vessels," p. 619; Bancroft, *California*, II: 708-709.

6 Valentín Gómez Farías (1781-1858) had been elected vice president in March 1833; Antonio López de Santa Anna, president. Since the latter would not come to Mexico City to take the oath of office, from April 1, Gómez Farías served as the acting chief executive. Thus he was in a powerful position to aid the plans for the California colony. However, by October Santa Anna had a change of heart and took the presidency. The vice president tried to resign, but Santa Anna refused his request. At the same time the president altered his cabinet which removed some supporters of the colonization scheme. Subsequently, Santa Anna retired to his hacienda in December and left the government for the time being in Gómez Farías's hands. Santa Anna finally forced Gómez Farías out of office and he went into exile to New Orleans with his family in September 1834. Hutchinson, *Frontier Settlement in Mexican California*, pp. 159-161, 194, 207-208, 214.

7 The expedition was financed solely from funds derived from the Mexican government which utilized income from the Pious Fund, a philanthropic endowment established in 1697 to support Jesuit missionary activity in Baja California. In 1834 it was sequestered by the government. Even en route more funds were appropriated for the colonists. There was no need for Híjar to sell his rancho as alluded to by Coronel (he mortgaged it). *Ibid.*, pp. 186-187, 204-205, 214-215.

8 The *Natalia*, commanded by Captain Juan Gómez, was a 195-ton Peruvian brig. Juan Bandini served as supercargo. It was purchased by a group of the colonists, not the Cosmopolitan Company. It sailed from San Blas on August 1 reaching Monterey on December 4, 1834, carrying 129 colonists as well as Híjar. On board also was José Noriega de la Guerra, who disembarked at San Diego on September 1st. The ship stayed in that port until November 21 when it sailed north. On December 21 the vessel was wrecked at Monterey. The companion ship, the *Morelos*, a 195-ton Mexican brig, commanded by Lucas F. Manso, sailed the same day as the *Natalia* with Padrés and about 100 colonists as passengers. It reached Monterey on September 24, 1834. Ogden, "Trading Vessels," pp. 674-675. However, the story of Napoleon being associated with the *Natalia*, "like a good many other traditional stories connected with the colony, is untrue." Hutchinson, *Frontier Settlement in Mexican California*, p. 204.

9 Serrano was accompanied by his wife, a widowed sister and her five children. There were two single Aguilars, José María and Santiago. The roster of the colonists is given in Ibid., Appendix D, pp. 419-422.

10 Augustín Janssens was also a passenger on the *Morelos* and later wrote his recollections which were published as *The Life and Adventures in California of Don Augustín Janssens, 1834-1856*, edited by William H. Ellison and Francis Price (San Francisco, 1955).

11 Coronel is not precise here. Vice President Gómez Farías had moved to appoint Híjar as successor to Figueroa as governor, but when Santa Anna was elected president, he countermanded the appointment. Subsequently, Gómez Farías decided to split the civil and military power in California, appointing Híjar as military commandant. It was this action that Santa Anna nullified in his July 25, 1834 communication to Figueroa. Hutchinson, *Frontier Settlement in Mexican California*, pp. 184, 187-188, 194-195, 265.

12 Mission San Jose had been secularized and was then in the custody of Vallejo, the military commandant of the Sonoma District.

13 It would appear that Coronel's views are somewhat biased. It is true that new colonists from Sonora had plotted and executed a rebellion in early March 1834 in Los Angeles, but it ended rather abruptly. However, two of the key figures were Padrés-Híjar colonists, Dr. Francisco Torres and Antonio Apalátequi, a Spanish clerk en route to Mexico with dispatches from Híjar. Figueroa, already highly suspicious of possible seditious sentiment among the new Mexican arrivals, his suspicions fed by a reputed mole, moved swiftly, ordering Vallejo to nip the rebellion in the bud on March 16. The few weapons and small ammunition rounded up could hardly have been called a dire threat. Figueroa's actions spelled the end of the Cosmopolitan Company and the Padrés-Híjar California venture. Bancroft, *California*, III: 281-288; Hutchinson, *Frontier Settlement in Mexican California*, pp. 326-328, 358-359, 363-364; Pío Pico, *Don Pío Pico's Historical Narrative*, translated by Arthur P. Botello, edited by Martin Cole and Henry Welcome (Glendale, Calif., 1973), pp. 60-63.

14 The names here need to be clarified. Those expelled on the *Santa Rosa*, a 425-ton Sardinian frigate, commanded by Captain Nicholas Bianchi, included: Padrés and Híjar, Francisco Torres, Antonio Apalátegui, Manuel María Gonzáles, José Mariano Romero (a teacher, not a lawyer), Nicanor Estrada, and Buenaventura Araujo, a naval officer. The name "Verousco" does not appear in the colonists' roster; possibly this was Francisco Berduzco (sometimes spelled Verduzco), age twenty-two, a merchant, not an officer.

15 There is no solid evidence to support Coronel in his appraisal of Santa Anna's motives.

16 Ramírez, who was apparently a friend of Gómez Farías, was appointed to his post in June 1833 as administrator of maritime customs. He became an outspoken critic of the colony on the grounds that its intention was to "reduce commerce to a system that would benefit only the Company called the Cosmopolitan," which would result in a "ruinous monopoly" in trade and commerce. This caught Figueroa's attention and no doubt exerted a strong influence on his anti-colony attitude so ably expressed in his manifesto. Hutchinson, *Frontier Settlement in Mexican California*, pp. 330-331, 334 (for quotes).

17 José Figueroa, *Manifesto to the Mexican Republic which Brigadier General José Figueroa, Commandant and Political Chief of Upper California presents on his conduct and on that of José María Híjar and José María Padrés as Directors of Colonization in 1834 and 1835*, translated and edited by C. Alan Hutchinson (Berkeley, 1978), *passim*.

18 Quite obviously, Coronel is decidedly biased on this subject for there is no evidence of Santa Anna's negativism as expressed by him, nor is Figueroa's *Manifesto* without factual evidence.

19 On January 15, 1833, with the arrival of Governer Figueroa, the California mission chain was split into two departments, one headed by Fr. Narciso Durán, headquartered at Mission Santa Barbara, and those missions from San Miguel north under the jurisdiction of Francisco García Diego y Moreno, destined to be California's first bishop. The distinction was that the former friars were from the College of San Fernando (Spanish) in Mexico City; the latter were from the College of Zacatecas (Mexican). García Diego was at this time in residence at Mission San Carlos Borremeo (Carmel) along with José María del Refugio Suárez del Real, a fellow Zacatecan friar who served there until 1843. Maynard Geiger, *Franciscan Missionaries in Hispanic California, 1769-1848* (San Marino, Calif., 1969), p. 249.

20 The allusion here is to the process of secularization of the California missions, 1833-35.

21 Only 142 Franciscans served in California prior to 1848. *Ibid*, p. vii.

Chapter 2.

1 Bancroft, *California*, II:759, provides the answer. He writes: Chico "appointed gov. of Cal. Dec. '35, arriving in April '36 ... and assuming his office May 2nd. He encountered bitter prejudice against Mex. rulers, and his position was made so uncomfortable by an unmanageable deputation and other soi-disant opponents of centralism that he was virtually forced to depart in Aug., his rule ending July 31."

2 Gutiérrez was overthrown by a rebellion headed by native son Juan B. Alvarado, greatly aided by José Castro. He was forced from office by him on November 4, 1836. For details of the rebellion, see *Ibid.*, III; 445-466.

3 The mainstay of Alvarado and Castro's endeavor was the company of American riflemen assembled by Isaac Graham, former fur trapper who settled in California in 1833. Associated with him in that

enterprise were William R. Garner and John Coppinger, both lieutenants under Graham's captaincy. Doyce B. Nunis, Jr., *The Trials of Isaac Graham* (Los Angeles, 1967), pp. 21-22; Bancroft, *California*, II: 766.

4 Gutiérrez surrended on November 5, 1836. He was sent packing with others on the brig *Clementine* in November which took him as far as Cabo San Lucas in Baja California. Bancroft, *California*, III: 467-477; Ogden, "Trading Vessels," pp. 729-730.

5 November 7, the deputation took its initial action, followed by making Alvarado the new governor, the first native-born Californian to hold that position.

6 All of this is detailed in Bancroft, *California*, III: 481-494, and in George Tays, "Revolutionary California: The Political History of California During the Mexican Period, 1822-1845" (Ph.D. Dissertation, University of California, Berkeley, 1934), pp. 381-411.

7 The Mexican Congress raised Los Angeles to the status of a city (*ciudad*) on May 25, 1835. (Broadside in the possession of the author.) This was achieved by José Antonio Carrillo, but it took place earlier than reported by Coronel who implies 1838.

8 Las Flores, also called San Pedro, is marked today by fragmentary ruins of an adobe built by the mission fathers about 1823. It served as a hospice for travelers between Missions San Luis Rey (to the south) and San Juan Capistrano (to the north). Later it became a *ranchería* for the neophytes of Mission San Luis Rey in 1833. Today, the site is within the confines of the U.S. Marines' Camp Pendleton. William N. Abeloe, ed., *Historic Spots in California* (3rd ed., Stanford, 1966), p. 335; Bancroft, *California*, III: 339.

9 The principal negotiators were Governer Carrillo and Juan Bautista Alvarado: the date was April 21, 1837. They were related; Alvarado was Carrillo's nephew. This helps explain why bloodshed was avoided; many of the participants on both sides were related by kinship. Bancroft, *California*, III: 559.

10 Coronel's memory here is faulty. Originally, no prisoners were taken at Las Flores. All were allowed to return to Los Angeles, while Alvarado returned north. However, the Carrillo faction commenced to plot and plan again. This led to their arrest on May 20 by a group of Los Angeles citizens. At the same time, Alvarado sent a detachment of twenty-five men from Santa Barbara under the command of José Ramón Villavicencio to put a stop to any conspiracy. Those arrested included Carlos and José Antonio Carrillo, Pío Pico, Gil Ibarra, Narciso Botello, Ignacio Palomares, and José A. Ramírez. Re-arrested were Andrés Pico and Ignacio del Valle and Roberto Parado at Santa Barbara. The prisoners were marched to Santa Barbara for confinement. Pío Pico, being quite ill, served a short sentence in the presidio, while Carlos Carrillo was paroled on the condition he cease to be involved in politics. The rest were marched north to Sonoma and confined there by Commandant General Vallejo from June 3 to "the end of September, or a little later." *Ibid.*, pp. 565-567.

11 Castillero sailed for Mexico on the *California* in the middle of August, reaching Acapulco on September 15, 1837. He returned to Monterey on November 15, 1838. *Ibid.*, pp. 531, 574.

Chapter 3.

1 Bancroft states that José Castro was appointed prefect of the first district, while Cosmé Peña's appointment was not approved by Mexico. Alvarado was acting under the Mexican laws of December 30, 1836 and March 20, 1837. *Ibid.*, pp. 685-686.

2 The time span here would be from 1831 to 1840.

3 Coronel is actually describing the hide and tallow trade which did not commence on any significant scale until 1828. Certainly between 1828-1840 the trade was a significant factor in the economic life of California, including the missions. However, secularization began in 1833. It was with secularization that the vast cattle herds of the missions vanished. The best study of this aspect of California's history is found in Sherman F. Dallas, "The Hide and Tallow Trade in Alta California, 1822-1846" (Ph.D. Dissertation, Indiana University, 1955).

4 The reference here is to the so-called "Graham Affair," named after Isaac Graham, an American who settled in California in 1833. On April 7, 1840, Governor Alvarado ordered his arrest along with a number of other foreigners, American and English. In all, forty-seven were sent to Mexico on April 23 to stand trial for treason. After intervention by the British and U.S. governments, the prisoners were released and returned to Monterey on July 20, 1841. This affair is discussed in detail in Nunis, *The Trials of Isaac Graham*, pp. 22-30. Also, see Bancroft, *California*, IV: 11-34.

5 The trial lasted from the end of 1840 until May 1841. The charges of cruelty and inhumane treatment of the Graham Affair prisoners were leveled by the British and American ministers. Upon his aquittal, Castro returned overland to California, reaching the province in September. *Ibid.*, p. 34.

6 The last statement is inaccurate. Only later was Graham compensated for his imprisonment and treatment, as well as loss of property. He was the only one who persevered in the quest for indemnification. He finally received a payment of $38,125 in 1851. Nunis, *The Trials of Isaac Graham*, pp. 33-45.

7 Micheltorena's appointment was dated January 22, 1842, one which gave him both civil and military power. The number of his battalion was fixed at 500, 200 to be regular soldiers, 300 hundred prisoners. The rest of Coronel's comments are true. The company sailed in four ships from Mazatlán on July 25 and reached San Diego on August 25. Bancroft, *California*, IV: 286-290.

8 Actually, the deserters were not sent to California until two years later. *Ibid.*, p. 289.

9 He arrived in Los Angeles for the gala fiesta on September 25. *Ibid.*, pp. 290-292n. Coronel in his memoir mistakenly uses October.

10 Actually, to avoid the transfer of power personally, Alvarado appointed Jimeno acting governor who installed Micheltorena on December 30. Accompanying Jimeno south, in addition to those mentioned, were Rafael Gonzáles and Zenón Fernandez. *Ibid.*, p. 294.

11 Jones seized Monterey on October 20, but returned it the following day in the mistaken belief that the U.S. and Mexico were at war. *Ibid.*, pp. 307-311.

12 Jones's meeting with Micheltorena in Los Angeles took place on January 18 at the adobe of Abel Stearns; the conference was held on the 19th; a banquet that night as described by Coronel, with Jones and his officers departing on January 21. *Ibid.*, pp. 320-323. The Rancho Cuenos was probably the Rancho San Pedro for the *Cyane*, Jones's ship, lay at anchor off its coast.

13 José Limantour came to Micheltorena's aid in early 1843. For his assistance he was paid in land grants, which later became much entangled in fraud and a famous trial. Kenneth M. Johnson, *José Yvez Limantour v. the United States* (Los Angeles, 1961), *passim*.

14 General Alvarez was able to persuade the men to join him in the December 1843 revolution against President José Joaquín de Herrara, along with all the stores and ships. Bancroft, *California*, IV: 529.

Chapter 4.

1 José L. Sepúlveda was appointed sub-prefect for Los Angeles on July 12, 1845 at a yearly salary of $600, "which he deemed too little. The assembly refused to raise the salary and S[epúlveda] seems to have taken the office unwillingly, and perhaps resigned, as the place was offered in Oct[ober] to A[ntonio] F. Coronel." He declined as noted in his narrative. Abel Stearns was appointed to the office on June 17, 1846 and was sworn on June 20. Bancroft, *California*, IV: 633 *note*; V: 624 *note*.

2 On February 1, 1845, Pío Pico, as president of the revolutionary junta meeting in Los Angeles, moved to "appoint a committee to wait on Micheltorena, to consult with him on means for putting an end to dissentions" so as to avoid bloodshed. On the third, the following were appointed to this peace commission: Coronel, José Antonio de la Guerra of Santa Barbara, Antonio M. Lugo, Vincent Sánchez, and Abel Stearns. *Ibid*, V: 487-498. John Wilson was not a member of the negotiating committee.

3 The meeting was held on February 7. *Ibid.*, p. 498.

4 Castro was in San Buenaventura; Alvarado was en route south with reinforcements at this date. *Ibid.*, pp. 501-502. It is quite clear Alvarado was not in San Buenaventura at this time; therefore what follows is partially inaccurate. Alvarado did rejoin Castro in Los Angeles around February 17.

5 Since Wilson and Alvarado were not participants in these negotiations, one must discount that portion of Coronel's recollections as faulty memory. Also, Bancroft does not indicate any subsequent meetings after the initial one on February 7th between the peace committee and Micheltorena. Possibly Coronel's recollection of the general's private conversation with him took place on February 7, not in a later visit.

Chapter 5.

1 Micheltorena's force entered San Buenaventura on February 15. Reputedly some cannon shots were fired at Castro's retreating force. *Ibid.*, pp. 501-502.

2 Micheltorena's foreign contingent began to desert his cause while he was at the Rincon west of San Buenaventura; the rest were persuaded to depart during a negotiation carried out by Benjamin D. Wilson (whom Coronel has probably confused with John Wilson of Santa Barbara) at Cahuenga Pass, accompanied by Pío Pico and Narciso Botello. The Treaty of Cahuenga was signed on February 22. *Ibid.*, pp. 505-509; "Benjamin David Wilson's Observations on Early Days in California and New Mexico," *Annual Publication Historical Society of Southern California*, XVI, Pt. 1 (1934): 97-101.

3 The general and his troops were marched to San Pedro soon after the capitulation at Cahuenga. There they encamped for about two weeks at the Rancho Palos Verdes near San Pedro. They then boarded the chartered *Don Quixote*, sailing for Monterey on March 12. On arrival at Monterey on March 19, no troops were allowed to land. The rest of the garrison was ordered aboard, along with the general's wife, and the vessel sailed to Mexico at the end of March, reaching San Blas by April 19, 1845. Bancroft, *California*, IV: 511-512.

4 José L. Sepúlveda was appointed sub-prefect on July 12, 1845, at a salary of 600 *pesos*. Finding this inadequate, he may have tried to resign, for in October Coronel was offered the post but declined. José

Ramón Argüello was appointed to the post on April 3, 1846. With the coming of the U.S. armed forces with the Mexican War, Stearns was appointed as indicated by Coronel. *Ibid.*, p. 633*n*, V: 632*n*.

5 The plot was planned for November 28, but Pico nipped it in the bud. Carrillo and Hilario Varela, Sérbulo's brother, were exiled to Mexico, sailing on the *Clarita*. Sérbulo was detained in prison, but escaped before the end of the year. All three exiles returned early in 1846. *Ibid.*, IV: 540-541.

6 McNamara approached the Mexican government in August 1845 with his colonization scheme, which was received favorably. To press the matter, he sailed to Monterey on H.M.S *Juno*, reaching there the middle of June. He informed Thomas O. Larkin, the U.S. consul, of his plan as well as others before departing for Santa Barbara to call on Bishop García Diego and Governer Pico. On July 1 he submitted his proposal to Pico who in turn presented it to the assembly in Los Angeles. A committee report reacted favorably with certain restrictions. But the Mexican War erupted and the project was doomed. *Ibid.*, V: 216-220.

7 Híjar came as a commissioner, acting on instructions dated April 11, 1846 from the Mexican government, which in essence sanctioned the Pico revolt and the *status quo* in California. In the meantime, the government was planning to send a punitive expedition to right matters its way, a plan that never matured. Híjar reached Santa Barbara on June 8 and was well received by Pico and the departmental government. The intervention of war brought an end to his mission rather abruptly. In frail health, he died on December 19 and was buried the following day in the graveyard of the Plaza Church in Los Angeles. *Ibid.*, IV: 526-530*n*.

8 The Bear Flag Revolt took place on June 14, 1846. The two Vallejos and Prudhomme (sometimes spelled Prudon) were taken prisoner and sent to Sacramento as was Jacob R. Leese. They were detained at Sutter's Fort until late August when they were released. *Ibid.*, VI: 119; Fred B. Rogers, *William Brown Ide, Bear Flagger* (San Francisco, 1962), pp. 41-60.

9 Commodore John D. Sloat took possession of California at Monterey on July 7, 1846.

10 Naval forces reached San Pedro on August 6, 1846.

11 On the night of August 10, 1846, Pico and Castro left Los Angeles. Castro, accompanied by Francisco Arce, his secretary, and a few others took the Colorado River route overland to Sonora. Pico went south to his brother-in-law's ranch, Santa Margarita, near present-day Oceanside and hid out for a month. Forewarned about the prospect of capture, he headed south again for Baja California with his secretary José Matías Moreno, crossing the border on September 7; subsequently crossing the gulf to Guaymas, then on to Hermosilla. He returned to California in midyear,1848. Bancroft, *California*, V: 277-279.

Chapter 6.

1 Paredón Blanco was just outside of Los Angeles, the exact location not being known.

2 Coronel's Rancho Cañada Atras de los Verdugos lay north of present-day La Cañada and La Crescenta north of Los Angeles. Cowan, *Ranchos of California*, p. 107, No. 659.

3 This would be Fort Moore Hill, presently occupied by the Los Angeles Unified School District headquarters.

4 The three Callahan brothers were locally known as "Ein," "Epli," and "Geral," but two of them were

probably named Evan and Isaac; the third remains unknown. They reached California in 1846, so they were new arrivals. Roubidru was Louis Robidoux. Bancroft, *California*, III: 739.

5 There are conflicting accounts of the Battle of Rancho Chino. Coronel's account is fairly close to some, but is incorrect in several places: i) Isaac Williams' wife was a Lugo, but he was not dead; instead, he came out with his family for their safety; ii) three of the Americans were wounded, two seriously; iii) the Americans surrendered on September 28. *Ibid.*, V: 312-314; "Wilson's Observations," pp. 106-110; George W. Beattie, "Where Was the Battle of Chino Fought?" *Quarterly Historical Society of Southern California*, XXII (1940): 62-69, and his article, "The Battle of Chino," *Ibid.*, XXIV (1942): 143-163.

6 Gillespie was able to obtain passage on the merchant ship *Vandalia*, four or five days after camping on the San Pedro beach. Bancroft, *California*, III: 315.

Chapter 7.

1 Rancho Cuerbos or Cuervos lay northwest of the present city of Gardena in southwestern Los Angeles County. Cowan, *Ranchos of California*, p. 31, No. 139.

2 Coronel was witnessing the march of General Stephen W. Kearny's forces which had already taken control of New Mexico and were now moving to reinforce the armed forces in California.

Chapter 8.

1 Pala lies due east of Mission San Luis Rey and was a rancheria of that mission.

2 Temecula is situated in northern San Diego County.

3 Jackson, *Glimpses of the California Missions*, p. 201-206, provides a summary of the harrowing wartime experiences of Coronel.

4 Rancho Rincon de San Pasqual (or Pascual) included in its boundaries present-day Pasadena and Altadena. The reference here is actually to the Rancho Santa Margarita y Las Flores which spread from present-day San Onofre to San Luis Rey, south to Escondido. It was near the latter that the ensuing Battle of San Pasqual was fought on December 6, 1846. *Ibid.*, p. 86, No. 516 and p. 93, No. 566.

5 Rancho Coyotes was situated in and around the present-day city of Buena Park and straddled the Los Angeles - Orange County line. *Ibid.*, p. 30, No. 131.

Chapter 9.

1 The original Rancho San Antonio, located in Los Angeles County in an area now occupied by the towns of Lynwood, Bell, Montebello and Maywood, was granted to Antonio María Lugo. Felipe, one of his many sons, shared in that ownership. Cowan, *Ranchos of California*, pp. 71-72, No. 411.

2 The Capitulation of Cahuenga was negotiated by John C. Frémont and signed by Andrés Pico on behalf of Governer Pío Pico and Captain José María Flores on January 13, 1847.

3 The new slate of officers were elected and/or appointed for 1848. The municipal government continued to function throughout 1848. Bancroft, *California*, V: 626-627n.

4 The reference is to Frémont's court-martial trial, a highly controversial affair in the early history

of American California, which focused on the issue of who had military authority in the California theater, General Kearny or Frémont. Kenneth M. Johnson, *The Frémont Court Martial* (Los Angeles, 1968), *passim*.

Chapter 10.

1 "In 1827 or 1828, a neophyte, Estanislao, probably named for one of the two Polish saints called Saint Stanislaus, ran away from Mission San Jose and became the leader of a band of Indians in the San Joaquin Valley." From this is derived the name of the Stanislaus River and the present-day county. Erwin G. Gudde, *California Place Names* (3rd ed., Berkeley and Los Angeles, 1969), p. 320.

2 Better known as Stanislaus Diggings in Calaveras County, probably near Robinson's Ferry. "On October 7, 1848, Francisco Coronel...began working a claim near the Stanislaus River in a ravine in which Indians had discovered rich deposits. In three days he gathered about 134 ounces of gold with the help of two servants, land he worked with continued success for about a month." Erwin G. Gudde, *California Gold Camps* (Berkeley and Los Angeles, 1975), p. 334.

3 The point made here is that the experienced miners from Sonora taught the inexperienced how to locate potential gold-bearing sites.

4 Juan Manso and Andrés Pico did not purchase the former mission, rather they rented it for $1,200 after Governor Pío Pico's regulation of October 27, 1845, authorized the territorial junta's resolution of May 28, which approved the sale of three former missions and the renting of four others by private individuals. Bancroft, *California*, V: 588 and *note*.

Chapter 11.

1 Juan Nepomuceno Padilla received the four-league Rancho Roblar de la Miseria in 1845. It was located in present-day Sonoma County northwest of Petaluma. Cowan, *Ranchos of California*, p. 68, No. 388.

2 The Eldorado Hotel in Sonoma was built by Salvador Vallejo, Mariano G. Vallejo's brother. In 1849-1850 it was operated by a man named Randolph George Pearce, later a prominent lawyer in Petaluma. Robert D. Parmelee, *Pioneer Sonoma* (Sonoma, 1972), p. 121.

Chapter 14.

1 The Indian tribes mentioned were the Yumans of the Colorado River, including the Upland group. Amajanes is a variant of the Mohave and Coshanes (Cohoninos) is a variant for the Havasupai. Alfonso Ortiz, ed., *Handbook of North American Indians*, Vol. 10: *Southwest* (Washington, D.C., 1983), pp. 24, 69.

2 Slavery was prohibited by the Mexican constitutions of 1824 and 1828. It would appear that Californios ignored that proscription when it came to acquiring Indian servants.

3 The Indians mentioned here were Cocopas and Maricopas. *Ibid.*, pp. 83, 111.

Chapter 15.

1 Mission San Gabriel fell into terrible disrepute fifteen years after its secularization. It became a gathering place for the less desirable persons in the community. It boasted a saloon with gambling,and a house of prostitution. Bean was shot near the mission on Sunday night, November 7. Mortally

wounded, he died early on the morning of December 9, 1852. *Los Angeles Star*, November 13, 1852, p. 2, cl. 2.

2 Six men were arrested by the committee and turned over to the Vigilance Committee: "Eleulerio," Cipriano Sandoval (a poor cobbler at Mission San Gabriel), Juan Rico, Reyes Feliz (or Felix), Jose Alviso, and Felipe Reid. The first five were tried, convicted, and sentenced to hang. Felipe Reid, no doubt because his stepfather was Hugo Reid, a longtime Los Angeles area resident, was turned over to the law, but was never tried. A contempory witness to the proceedings, trials, and executions expressed the opinion that Felipe Reid was the actual murderer, while Bancroft, without mentioning names, states the murderer confessed his crime on his death bed. *Ibid.*, November 27, 1852, p. 2, cl. 2; Horace Bell, *Reminiscences of a Ranger* (Santa Barbara, 1927), pp. 27-29; Hubert H. Bancroft, *Popular Tribunals* (2 vols., San Francisco, 1887), I: 493.

3 Dr. David W. Alexander was charged with the custody of these vigilante prisoners. *Los Angeles Star*, November 27, 1852, p. 2, cl. 2.

4 These executions are described in Bell, *Reminiscences of a Ranger*, pp. 28-29. The date was November 28, 1852.

5 Juan Flores, who had been with Murieta (or Murrieta), was hung by the townspeople on Fort Moore Hill in Los Angeles on February 14, 1857, for being the leader of a gang that murdered Sheriff James B. Barton and three of his posse on January 30, 1857. Marjorie T. Wolcott, ed., *Pioneer Notes From the Diaries of Judge Benjamin Hayes, 1849-1875* (Los Angeles, 1929), p. 160n.

6 He was caught on January 19, 1856.

7 Lawyers Kimball H. Dimmick, Cameron E. Thon, and Columbus Sims took turns defending Pancho Daniel after his arrest. He was brought to trial before Judge Benjamin Hayes in Los Angeles but was seized by vigilantes and summarily hung on November 30, 1858. W. W. Robinson, *Lawyers of Los Angeles* (Los Angeles, 1959), p. 46; Wolcott, ed., *Pioneer Notes*, p. 160n.

8 Coronel's recollection here is faulty. Dr. Wilson W. Jones was returning to Los Angeles from a professional call and "at about sunset, [he] nearly rode over the bleeding and still warm body of a cattle-buyer named Porter, on Alameda Street [in Los Angeles]. The latter had been out to the Dominguez *rancho* [San Pedro], to purchase stock, and had taken along with him a Mexican named Manuel Vergara who introduced himself as an experienced interpreter and guide, but who was, in reality, a cutthroat with a record of one or two assassinations. Vergara observed that Porter possessed a considerable amount of money; and on their way back to Los Angeles shot the American from behind." Jones quickly sounded the alarm and a volunteer police force pursued the culprit for about ninety miles. Having exhausted their ammunition, Vergara turned on one of the volunteers, cut his bridle and escaped. However, he was intercepted by a detachment of U.S. cavalry at Yuma under the command of Major Henry Heintzelman. Overtaken, Vergara was shot dead. Newmark, *Sixty Years*, p. 35; Bell, *Reminiscences of a Ranger*, pp. 103, 150-154.

Chapter 16.

1 The ex-convict was Andrés Fontes, the brother of a Capistrano Indian woman who had been Sheriff James R. Barton's mistress. The woman decided to leave the sheriff and moved to an Indian village east of Los Angeles. When Barton tried to regain his lost love, the brother intervened and a fight ensued. "Two days later the sheriff arrested Andrés on a charge of horse stealing, had him indicted, tried, convicted, and sent to San Quentin for two years." Fontes avowed his innocence and swore

vengeance, which he took subsequently on Barton and his small posse near San Juan Capistrano, after his release from prison. (See the notes which follow that detail what befell Barton and his men.) Horace Bell, *On the Old West Coast, Being Further Reminiscences of a Ranger*, edited by Lanier Bartlett (New York, 1930), pp. 72-74.

2 Eventually, the Daniel-Flores gang may have numbered as many as fifty-two. Bell, *Reminiscences of a Ranger*, p. 208.

3 Sheriff James Barton received the intelligence that there were robbers in the vicinity of San Juan Capistrano from the brother of Garnet Hardy, a Los Angeles teamster who had driven a delivery of goods to that small town south of the city. Advised that the robbers were in the vicinity, he wrote his brother, Alfred, who in turn informed the sheriff. The posse consisted of six men and was joined by a Frenchman (name not given, but here supplied by Coronel) as a guide. The gang robbed three stores and one house in San Juan Capistrano. In robbing the store of Charles Flugard on January 22, 1857, "they brutally murdered him in his own room, and then ordered his assistant to serve up supper for them on the counter, where they deliberately ate it, the dead body lying before them all the time." Robert G. Clelland, *Cattle on a Thousand Hills* (San Marino, 1964), p. 261. Newmark, *Sixty Years*, p. 206, states the murdered man was a German named Charles W. Pflugardt. Clelland reprints on pp. 250-263 the *verbatim* accounts from the *Los Angeles Star* relating to this entire episode.

4 The site was "about a mile down the Rodeo de la Laguna, on the rancho of San Joaquin, on the near side of the small hills to the right of Arroyo de los Palos Verdes -- on the Sanjon del Alisal -- about fifteen miles this side of the Mission of San Juan Capistrano." The date was January 30, 1857. Clelland, *Cattle on a Thousand Hills*, p. 253.

5 Barton and his two constables, Baker and Little, fell within 100 yards of each other, while the blacksmith, Charles F. Daly, was found three miles farther on in the middle of the Santa Ana road. The bodies were stripped of valuables, including boots and hats. *Ibid.*, p. 253.

6 Andrés Pico raised in all a company of fifty-one men. He set out originally from Los Angeles on January 26, 1857, with only nineteen, but picked up other recruits along the way to San Juan Capistrano. " ... [On] capturing Silvas and Ardillero, two of the worst of the *bandidos*, after a hard resistance, he straightway hung them to trees, at the very spot where they had tried to assassinate him and his companions." "Flores was caught on the top of a peak in the Santiago range; all in all some fifty-two culprits were brought to Los Angeles and lodged in jail; and of that number, eleven were lynched or legally hung." *Ibid.*, p. 255; Newmark, *Sixty Years*, p. 223.

7 Pancho Daniel made good his escape, going north to San Luis Obispo. He was captured in a haystack near San Jose by Sheriff John M. Murphy on January 19, 1858 and brought back to Los Angeles. After he was jailed, then released on bail, his lawyers secured a change of venue to Santa Barbara. A vigilante group intervened and on the morning of November 30, 1858, Daniel's "body was found hanging by the neck at the gateway to the County Jail yard ... " Newmark, *Sixty Years*, p. 223. The *Los Angeles Star*, December 4, 1858, p. 2, cl. 2, recounts in full the end of Pancho Daniel.

8 Vincente Sánchez came to Los Angeles at the age of nineteen in 1814. He became very active in the political life of Mexican California and held a number of important posts, including *alcalde* (mayor) of Los Angeles on two different occasions. His grandson, Tómas, served as sheriff of Los Angeles County from September 7, 1859 to September 4, 1867. Bancroft, *California*, V: 711; George Shochat, "The Casa Adobe de San Rafael (The Sanchez Adobe) in Glendale, California," Part I, *Quarterly Historical Society of Southern California*, XXXII (1950): 280-283.

9 Joseph Lancaster Brent (1826-1905) was much beloved and respected by the Californios. After arriving in California in 1850, he set himself to learning Spanish. On settling in Los Angeles, he opened a law practice and quickly became *the lawyer* for the local Spanish-speaking community. One of his most famous cases was the defense of several members of the Lugo family charged with murder, a trial which ended in acquittal for his clients. He also became the principal attorney for Californios in defending their land claims before the U.S. Land Commission. Robinson, *Lawyers of Los Angeles*, pp. 33-36; Newmark, *Sixty Years*, p. 46; Joseph L. Brent, *The Lugo Case* (New Orleans, 1926), *passim*.

10 Newmark writes: "Little San Gabriel, in which J. F. Burns, as Deputy Sheriff, was on watch ... [with] some of its people captured and executed three or four of Daniels' and Flores' band." There is no mention of the ghoulish act Coronel reports nor does the *Los Angeles Star* account refer to it either. Newmark, *Sixty Years*, p. 208.

11 Hilliard P. Dorsey's death was described as follows: "[He] was killed ... by his father-in-law, William Rubottom ... After quarreling with Rubottom, Dorsey, who was not a bad fellow, but had a fiery temper, had entered the yard with a knife in his hand; and Rubottom had threatened to shoot him if he came any nearer. The son-in-law continued to advance; and Rubottom shot him dead." Rubottom's lawyer was present at his El Monte home when this tragedy took place, a tragedy provoked by Dorsey's treatment of his wife, Rubottom's daughter. *Ibid.*, p. 144.

12 Coronel's bias is showing here. Dr. William B. Osborne (Osburn or Osbourne, variants) was a widely respected citizen of Los Angeles until his death in 1867. He held numerous public offices, some elective, some appointive; was enterprising in business and a man unafraid of launching new ventures. *Ibid.*, pp. 94, 138, 155, 192, 194. Newmark makes no reference to Dr. Osborne's being a cripple.

13 Coronel's allegation has not been verified.

14 Coronel's memory of this event is confused. On February 22, 1852, in honor of Washington's birthday, Abel Stearns hosted a fancy ball with a large number of invited guests, among them the two lawyers, James B. Watson and Myron Norton, both of whom were fortunately carrying arms. Around 11p.m. a crowd of men gathered at a barroom down the street from the Stearns adobe, denouncing "the givers of the ball as aristocrats" for not inviting the general public. They seized an old cannon from the plaza and wheeled it to Stearns's front door; then fired a cannon ball through the transom, which shattered and scattered the glass and panicked the women. Watson and Norton, armed, went to the door to confront the mob, but were met with "pistol shots, ringing gongs, fire crackers and a volley of abuse." Watson courageously, "sallied out [the door] alone ... [he] discharged four shots from the door, the effects of which were mortal wounds to Elias Cook and Dr. J. T. Overstreet. The mob then fled, leaving their wounded upon the ground." Joseph L. Brent was in attendance at the ball and after the shooting invited Norton (who was not wounded) and Watson to return with him to his rented quarters in the Ignacio del Valle adobe, an invitation which was accepted. The latter two were indicted. After a two day trial, they were acquitted. Judge Benjamin Hayes ruled their actions were "justifiable homicide under our laws." Judson A. Grenier, *California Legacy: The Watson Family* (N.P, 1987), pp. 85-89. Coronel is correct: the incident ceased as abruptly as it had erupted. However, Brent did not play any role as mediator or intervener.

Chapter 17.

1 Secularization, which was put into effect between 1833-35, literally ruined the once flourishing missions of California. The rationale behind the policy has long been argued as to the pros and cons. An insightful treatment is found in Manuel P. Servín, "The Secularization of the California Missions: A Reappraisal," *Southern California Quarterly*, XLVII (1965): 133-150.

2 Edith B. Webb in her book, *Indian Life at the Old Missions* (Reprint ed., Lincoln, Nebr., 1982), p. 54, recounts that a copy of a book published in Madrid, 1777, *Agricultura General*, found its way to a Franciscan missionary stationed at La Soledad. That copy is now in the Santa Barbara Mission Archive Library; another copy is in the library at the University of Santa Clara. But more importantly, Mrs. Webb writes as follows: "... in 1883, Helen Hunt Jackson found in Don Antonio Coronel's library...'a quaint old volume called 'Secrets of Agriculture, Fields and Pastures,' written by a Catholic Father in 1617, reprinted in 1781... " Mrs. Webb suggests that this book was originally in the library of Mission San Fernando, but more likely, in view of the remark below, it was from Mission San Gabriel. She further notes that in the 1835 inventories for Mission La Purisima and Santa Ines a book entitled *Secretos Agricultura* was listed.

In the Coronel Collection at the Los Angeles County Museum of Natural History there is a note which details the book in question. It was, indeed, entitled *Libro de los secretos de agricultura, casa de campo y pastores (Book of the Secrets of Agriculture, Fields and Pastures)*. It was translated from the Castellan by Father Miguel Agustín in the Priory of Fidelity of Perpinan, of the Religious Order of San Juan of Jerusalem, in 1617. It was printed in Madrid, 1761, by Joachín Ibarra. A further note states that Coronel received the copy from Fr. Zalvidea when he was stationed at Mission San Gabriel. Coronel Collection, No. 1568-1569. Unfortunately, the book is not in the collection any more.

3 Agustín Janssens came to California as a colonist with the Padrés-Híjar party in 1834, thus a fellow traveler with Coronel. He was appointed majordomo of Mission San Juan Capistrano by Fr. José María Zalvidea, who in that same year took temporary charge of temporalities. Janssens served in that capacity until the middle of 1841 when he relocated to Santa Barbara. Bancroft, *California*, IV: 624-625; Ellison and Price, eds., *The Life and Adventures in California of Don Agustín Janssens*, pp. 106-111.

4 Janssens also relates Fr. Zalvidea's behavior, but opines that "he was of a sane mind." *Ibid.*, p. 109. The discipline (a short three or four-strand rope with knots in it) was used widely by religious in the nineteenth century, especially the Franciscans. For a detailed discussion, see Francis F. Guest, "An Inquiry into the Role of the Discipline in California Mission Life," *Southern California Quarterly*, LXXXI (1989): 1-68.

5 El Molino Viejo, the first grist mill to be built in California, lies two miles north of Mission San Gabriel not far from the present-day Huntington Library in San Marino. It was built by Claudio López under the supervision of Fr. José María Zalvidea sometime between 1810 and 1812. The old mill building still stands and is a registered historic landmark. Abeloe, ed., *Historic Spots in California*, p. 147.

6 One of the things introduced into mission Indian life by the missionaries was music. Talented neophytes were taught to play instruments and to sing. They were taught both wind and string instruments. Under Fr. Narciso Durán, "the greatest of the missionary musicians who resided at Santa Barbara between 1833 and 1846...music and singing flourished." Maynard Geiger, *Mission Santa Barbara, 1782-1965* (Santa Barbara, 1965), p. 69.

7 One of the best descriptions of native medicine and medicine men is found in *As the Padres Saw Them*, edited by Maynard Geiger and Clement W. Meighan (Santa Barbara, 1976), pp. 71-80.

Chapter 21.

1 Since California was served by Franciscan priests from its founding in 1769, the traditions and practices of those friars had a strong influence on local customs. Burial was not in a Franciscan habit, but rather a shroud styled like it. The placement of the dying person on the floor was likened to the action requested by Saint Francis of Assisi, the Franciscan founder, when he lay dying.